happy
lawyer

*The Art of
Having It All
Without Losing
Your Mind*

Beverly *and* Dirk Davidek

NEW YORK

LONDON • NASHVILLE • MELBOURNE • VANCOUVER

happy lawyer

Published in New York, New York, by Morgan James Publishing in partnership with Difference Press.
www.MorganJamesPublishing.com

The Morgan James Speakers Group can bring authors to your live event. For more information or to book an event visit The Morgan James Speakers Group at
www.TheMorganJamesSpeakersGroup.com.

ISBN 978-1-68350-752-9 paperback
ISBN 978-1-68350-753-6 eBook
Library of Congress Control Number: 2017913736

Cover Design by:	**Interior Design by:**
Rachel Lopez	Megan Whitney
	Creative Ninja Designs
	megan@creativeninjadesigns.com

In an effort to support local communities, raise awareness and funds, Morgan James Publishing donates a percentage of all book sales for the life of each book to Habitat for Humanity Peninsula and Greater Williamsburg.

Get involved today! Visit
www.MorganJamesBuilds.com

For Johnnie Mae, Marlene, Gerard, Steven, and Nick.
We love you, always.

content

Foreword . . . . *vii*

Introduction *1*

Chapter 1 - Rae's Story 5

Chapter 2 - The BALANCED Way™ 11

Chapter 3 - Be True to Yourself 17

Chapter 4 - Ask and Allow 35

Chapter 5 - Let Go of What No Longer Serves You . . 51

Chapter 6 - Alkalize to Optimize 65

Chapter 7 - Nourish Your Body 83

Chapter 8 - Cleanse for Clarity 85

Chapter 9 - Exercise 107

Chapter 10 - Decide Your Path Forward 127

Chapter 11 - Embrace the Journey 139

Conclusion 159

Acknowledgements 167

About the Authors 173

Thank You 177

foreword

every day I speak to and hear from lawyers who have achieved some of the greatest heights of success in the world, and are miserable in their lives and lost, uncertain what to do next. After years of working so hard to be successful, and "making it" in the eyes of the world around us, how can "it" feel so bad?

I remember starting to have these thoughts around the age of 28 years old. I had graduated first in my class from Georgetown University Law Center, gotten married, had my first baby and been hired as an associate at one of the best law firms in the country. A $15,000 signing bonus, earning $165,000 my first year in practice, and able to afford and move into a starter home in Redondo Beach, California, I should have been in heaven. Or so I thought.

But I wasn't in heaven at all. Far from it.

I was miserable.

Each day, I would drag myself out of bed, leaving my husband and baby sleeping to make the hour plus commute to downtown Los Angeles. Several times a day, I would lock my door to pump breastmilk for my baby girl, who I missed terribly. And, oftentimes, her dad, who was staying home with her, would call me to tell me he couldn't get her to stop crying.

I felt helpless.

I worked all day on complex tax projects for a partner who liked to teach by trial, and I was fairly certain I was getting it wrong more often than I was getting it right. I thought I must be the stupidest person they ever hired.

On occasion, I would get to work with the estate planning partner, meeting with families and then searching and replacing our firm's form documents to create estate plans that were pretty much guaranteed to have mistakes and not even work when the clients needed them because we always stayed at the surface and never even inventoried the assets.

I knew the family would have a rough go of it, relying on the documents that were sure to be outdated when our clients died. But I didn't feel as if I had any real say in the matter, so I just kept doing as I was told. And I felt bad that I wasn't more grateful.

Truth be told, the firm truly was one of the good ones, as big law firms go. I had my own office with a lock on my door, so pumping breastmilk was easy. For the most part, other than the old-school partner who seemed to hate all of my work, everyone was really kind. And the pay was great, even though after taxes, insurance and my 401k, I only took home half of what I was paid.

Best of all, the firm let me take on my own clients, so long as they passed the conflicts check and I came to learn that this was quite rare in the world of big law. So instead of leaving, I decided I would make the best of my time there and build my own law practice within the big law firm.

That decision led me to attend the Manhattan Beach Women in Business Chamber of Commerce event in 2002. During that event, I heard a woman speaking about branding. But I didn't hear a word she said about branding.

What I heard was a vision of life that I wanted to step into.

She was a mom, she worked from home, and she loved her clients. She had full control over her schedule and a life she loved.

I wanted THAT!

I'd never even imagined something like that was possible. But as soon as I heard her speak, I knew that it was, and I wanted it. So I bought her book hoping I'd find some insights that would guide me. And I did.

Reading her acknowledgements like a scavenger seeking pearls (in this case pearls of wisdom), I found the name of a coach she had worked with to create her dream life and business. Immediately, I called that coach up and talked with her about hiring her.

Now, mind you, this was 2002, before everyone knew what coaching was and had a coach. Back then, coaching was still considered weird. At least in my book. And my mind was raging at me, "Alexis," it screamed "you don't need no stinking coach. You're way smarter than her. She didn't graduate first in her class from Georgetown."

Yep, those were the kinds of thoughts and mindset driving me back then.

Fortunately, I had some other, wiser voices guiding me as well and they said "Alexis, she may not have graduated first in her class from Georgetown, but she's happy with her life and business and, frankly, you can't say the same. Maybe there is something you can learn here." So I continued to think about working with this coach.

There was one huge part though that was standing in my way. It would require me to spend $350/month. On myself. On a coach for me.

I had never spent that kind of money on myself, unless you count the student loans I took on for law school. All my money went to the house, my husband, and my daughter. Heck, I was still wearing the suits I had bought for my job interviews, more than three years later. (Truth be told, I still wear those suits today, nearly twenty years later, because I so rarely wear a suit these days and I did buy some nice suits.)

But I knew I had to do it. I had to make the investment in discovering how to have a life and law practice I would love.

I knew I couldn't do it on my own because there was just too much I couldn't see that was keeping me stuck.

So, I did it. I said yes. I made the investment. Within two years, I had made the leap into my own law practice, not something I had ever considered possible (or even something I desired) when I first hired that coach.

Today, 15 years later, my life is radically different and exactly what I always dreamed it would be. I went on to build that law practice into a million dollar plus law firm in just three years by creating a new law business model.

And today, I get to work from home, on my own schedule, only working with clients I absolutely love (like Beverly who has written this book), exactly as I once envisioned I wanted to do when I heard that gal speak at the Chamber event.

The best part is that I didn't have to stop being a lawyer in order to do it.

I did need to get clear on the life I wanted, what was possible and then find the people who could step-by-step support and guide me to say yes to this life. None of it would have been possible if I had not seen other women I respected and admired go first.

That's why I am so grateful that Beverly and her husband Dirk have invested their time and energy in writing this book for you.

After reading it, you will have a clear vision of the life you want to have, as well as the next-step tools you'll need to create that life in, as Beverly and Dirk say, a BALANCED Way™.

That's the beginning.

Welcome to the journey toward a life worth living. You're in the right place.

Alexis Neely

Bestselling author of *Wear Clean Underwear!: A Fast, Fun, Friendly – and Essential – Guide to Legal Planning for Busy Parents* and founder of New Law Business Model™

introduction

"If I'm So Smart, Why Did I Become a Lawyer?"

i bet you've been miserable in your job for a long time. I bet you've had lots of ideas about which direction you should go with your career, whether those are ways to make more money, ways to relax more, ways to be your own boss, or ways to leave the profession.

Maybe you even spend time during the day when you're supposed to be working on an important deadline surfing the net, looking for other jobs, and/or reading travel blogs. Maybe you haven't done any of that, even though you would really like to, because ... who has time for that?

One thing I know from experience is that it takes an incredible amount of time and energy to find the right job. It truly is a balancing act, trying to keep all the plates spinning, trying to support yourself and your family, while you search for something that suits all of you better. Right-sizing your career can be about as easy as climbing Mount Everest.

A true career transformation can be daunting, to say the least. If you want to nail it, you've got to go all in – mind, body, and spirit. That's what this book is all about.

If you've been drawn to this book, I believe it's because it was truly meant for you. I believe you want something more out of your life. I suspect you have been yearning for fulfillment and struggling to be a happy lawyer for a long time.

That happy thing just keeps eluding you, no matter how hard you try to force it.

You want a career that allows you to feel good and do good; to become more than you are currently being; to honor yourself and others, especially your family; and to have fun.

Wouldn't that be nice?

I'm here to tell you that you can have all of that and more.

If you are ready to make profound changes in your life, this book is for you. I call it the BALANCED Way™ to practice law. It's an ongoing process, an art really, and one that you can learn, too.

I'll show you how.

I had to learn it the hard way, but you don't have to keep beating your head against the wall like I did. You're why I wrote this book.

I left the practice of law twice before deciding to become and embrace the lawyer I was meant to be. Along the way, I learned some invaluable lessons – about health and wellness, about other cultures, about love, and about what really matters. I certainly had a lot of help, and I put up a lot of resistance, but I finally got out of my own way and created a life that I love.

Before we jump in and help you create a life you love, I need to tell you that, although I am the one with the JD behind my name and many of the stories in this book are personal, I did not learn the contents of this book and become the happy lawyer on my own. Nor did I write this book on my own. Not even close.

My husband and co-author Dirk has been my inspiration, my biggest cheerleader, my business and accountability partner, and a whole lot more.

To help you, the reader, get through this information in an easy, readable manner, we've decided to write from the first person "I" most of the time. You'll read "Dirk's Corner" at the end of each step of the BALANCED Way™ process, but he has contributed much, much more to this book.

If ever anyone knew how to help a lawyer become a happy lawyer, it is Dirk.

Throughout the book we invite you to visit our website, www.happylawyerbook.com, for additional reading on particular topics. We both hope you will, as we both encourage you to keep moving towards the lawyer you were born to be.

Wishes come true.

Let's get to work on yours.

chapter one
Rae's Story

"I'm sure that a huge proportion of the situation you are facing, is out of your control. There's nothing you can do about it. But that proportion can't be 100 percent. There's got to be some proportion – let's say it's even just 2 percent – that is within your control. You can work on that. Who knows what a difference that may make!"

RICHARD N. BOLLES

On March 25, 2010, Rae walked away from her job as imbedded outside counsel for a major corporation. She hated that title, and she hated that job.

As of that day, Rae had been a lawyer for over 15 years. Throughout her career, she'd worked for a couple of small and mid-sized law firms, been an assistant DA, and been in solo practice. She had changed jobs more often than most lawyers she knew, always in the hopes of doing better for her family and always in the hopes of not losing her mind. It was a constant quest for more money and more peace of mind. She worked with and for some really great people. In some cases, she had mentors who without a doubt helped mold her into a very skilled lawyer. She also had some terrible, bordering on sadistic, supervisors who almost drove her away from the profession.

Almost.

Rae will tell you, she really didn't know what to expect from the beginning. Before she started law school, she didn't have any concept about what lawyering actually looked like. There were no other lawyers in her family, and her family had never had a "family lawyer." The topic of someone in her family needing a lawyer never even came up in conversation when she was growing up. In fact, her dad tried to talk her out of becoming a lawyer. To him, the supply far exceeded the demand, and he knew Rae was meant to be a writer.

Rae's first husband came from a family of lawyers. One day, way back when Rae had been out of college for about 18 months, was already married with a baby, and was plodding along as a middle school teacher, she had her in-laws over for dinner. She'd had a bad day at school, which isn't uncommon when you teach teenagers. But she was particularly stressed out that night, and the baby was unusually fussy. While she was flailing about trying to look like she had it all under control, her father-in-law at the time – a retired judge whom Rae highly respected – looked at her from over the top of the newspaper and proclaimed, "You're too smart to be a teacher. You should go to law school." And so it was.

Now, Rae knew from personal experience that most teachers are at least as smart as most lawyers. But in that moment, her ego needed a boost. And this was it. Most important, though, having a law degree meant she'd be able to help people and earn more money than as a teacher (she assumed). Rae was hard-wired to help people. Win-win.

So, here's what happened. Immediately upon passing the bar exam, Rae started noticing that the profession felt awfully elitist. That was not her thing at all. With the exception of a brilliant and exceedingly patient mentor with whom she shared office space, she didn't really like hanging out with the other lawyers she knew at that time. Many of them seemed like they were in it to look successful and make a lot of money just for the sake of making a lot of money, instead of genuinely wanting to help people.

She'd noticed some of that behavior in law school. She'd just thought that would get left behind when everyone graduated, grew up, and got real jobs. Rae had babies to take care of (her second son was born on her first day of class as a 2L), student loans to pay back, and a husband whose career was ramping up. She didn't have the time or desire to play those games.

Worse than that, though, Rae noticed that a lot of lawyers who'd been in the profession for a while seemed to be burning themselves out and were often bitter, unhealthy, and unhappy with their jobs. She wondered if she was just spending too much time at the courthouse and getting a skewed, pessimistic view. But she knew she did not want to become one of those lawyers.

Unfortunately, like many lawyers, Rae quickly grew to despise the practice of law. She hated all the bickering and pettiness that seemed to come with the territory. She hated it when opposing counsel purposely escalated matters just to run up fees, when divorce clients with kids spent their time and money arguing over things like who got the refrigerator, and when it felt like all that mattered at the end of each month was the total number of billable hours. "When do you get to do the helping people part?" she often wondered.

Fast-forward 15 years. A lot had happened, including her first marriage having "run its course," in the words of a local judge. Sure, there was a lot of heartache, guilt, and worry that initially ensued. But eventually, Rae felt like she got it all mostly together, and she learned to be content most of the time.

That job thing, though....

When Rae was corporate counsel, she finally slipped into a deep depression and tried to medicate her way into happiness. Like most people who suffer from depression, she hid it well – except from her husband and, probably, her sons. By now, Rae was married to Ron, her three sons were teens and a preteen, and all was going great in her life but for her stupid job. The legal profession as she knew it had her so crazed that it turned her into a person that she didn't even recognize. She'd been given the nickname "Bubbly" by some of her non-lawyer friends years ago, and not just because she liked champagne. She often wondered where that person went.

So one day, after a PA gave Rae a sample of an antidepressant to help her with her "blue" feeling, Rae spiraled way out of control. She ended up at her mom's house late that night, completely manic. She went there because she knew she wouldn't harm herself at Mom's. She bawled and bawled, telling her mom that Ron was going to leave her, and that she didn't blame him. Ron had never said this, but it was absolutely what Rae expected to happen. And she felt powerless to stop it. She was losing her mind.

She decided, "No more psychotropic drugs for me. Ever." But the problem persisted.

During the corporate counsel phase of her life, Rae also visited with a family counselor, intuitive coaches, and even a psychic. Some were better than others. None of them were lawyers, though, so she felt like none of them really got it. None of them could really help her.

Exhausted, Rae often daydreamed about napping on a warm, quiet beach somewhere like Fiji. When she had the time, she'd read travel blogs or search for other, better jobs. The grass was always greener, and she wondered what was wrong with her. How and when did she become this person? It always came back to, "I need to find a job that helps me provide for my family and allows me to be … me. And I need to find it now."

She was stuck. Trapped. She felt duped. She'd gone to law school for altruistic reasons, worked hard to support her family, thought she'd mostly done all the right things, and now she was utterly exhausted. She just didn't think she could do it anymore.

I suspect you can relate to much of what Rae was going through. I know I can.

Rae is me, and Ron is Dirk, before we learned what I'll teach you in the following pages.

Fasten your seatbelt, and let's get your life back.

It's time.

chapter two

The BALANCED Way™

"Happiness is not a matter of intensity but of balance, order, rhythm and harmony."

THOMAS MERTON

t took me more than two decades to figure this out, but when I was struggling with how much I detested my job and becoming a person I knew I was not meant to be, part of the problem was that I was suppressing my own creative, spiritual, and free-spirited side. I was out of rhythm for years. I needed my practice to be a true reflection of who I am as a person and what I came here to do. I needed to be in harmony with that girl.

Newsflash! You don't have to practice law in a way that feels out of balance with who you are, either. There's a better way, and that's your way. Becoming the lawyer you were born to be honors all of who you are: mind, body, and spirit. That's the BALANCED Way™. I call it the art of having it all without losing your mind because you get to create it and do it on your own terms.

Ready to get started? Here are the steps to achieving the legal career that you've dreamed of in a BALANCED Way™:

B — Be True to Yourself

The first step requires that you take some time to really get to know yourself. I know, you're busy taking care of everyone else. I get it. I'll try to make this as easy as possible because, frankly, you have to get this step down before anything else will work. Using the tools I give you in Chapter 3, you'll be able to identify your personality type and will have an idea about what types of jobs are, or are not, in alignment with your ultimate goal — to find a job that allows you to take care of your family without losing your mind, right? Got that.

A — Ask and Allow

Once you get to know yourself a little better, the next step is to go within, sit with what you know, and tap into your own intuition for guidance and clarity on your path forward. This is where two of my favorite books, *What Color Is Your Parachute* and *Ask and It Is Given*, converge, and it is a powerful practice. Your inner voice has been telling you that something's wrong. This step teaches you how to ask it for what's right and to allow the magic that will begin to happen.

L — Let Go of What No Longer Serves You

In this step of the process, you'll take note of beliefs and ways of doing things that no longer serve you or your family. This is where the rubber starts to meet the road, because you'll have to dig deep and make some tough decisions. You'll learn to identify what's been stopping you from having your dream job and what you can do to turn that around. It's not an easy thing to do, but I'll guide you through it.

A — Alkalize to Optimize

You're going to start to feel more empowered than you may have felt in years — if ever. You'll be ready to start really paying attention to what's happening with your body not just physically, but also mentally and spiritually, so you can squeeze more goodness out of each day. You'll recognize that one of your greatest assets as a lawyer is your health. I know you might not be ready to imagine it yet, but this step details how to get started at your own pace.

N — Nourish Your Body

Once you're feeling more empowered and are starting to feel better mentally and physically, you'll want to make sure you're providing your body with the nourishment that this profession demands — especially when you approach it from a holistic perspective. In this step, I'll provide you with what you need to know to have massive amounts of energy to conquer each day and to know that you're projecting the most vibrant, confident version of yourself to prospective employers, clients, and others. Taking charge of your career and your life in a BALANCED Way™ isn't always easy. But you'll be blown away by how much more fun it can be, and how much better you'll feel, when you get this step down.

C — Cleanse for Clarity

Even when you incorporate all the other steps in a BALANCED Way™, fatigue and illness can still set in. Of course, it's always important in life to keep your immune system strong. It's even more critical when you're going through a major life change like a career transition. This is where clean living comes in, and it's important. I'll give you the tools you need to do it. This is a step that so many otherwise healthy people overlook or fail to take seriously. But remember, your health is one of your greatest assets. I promise that when you incorporate this step into your routine, you'll have so much energy and clarity, you might even feel like a whole new person. And here's a bonus: your skin will glow, and your eyes will sparkle in a way you might not have seen in decades. You're going to feel younger, happier, and empowered.

E — Exercise

Okay, maybe you're a marathoner or maybe you never exercise. Most of us are somewhere in between. For me, exercise usually means getting outside and walking on the beach, or going for a hike in the woods. I also love yoga. Like most people, I go through periods when it feels hard to prioritize exercise. I understand that when you're going through a transition, and perhaps incorporating new lifestyle choices along the way, it can be challenging to make the time to exercise on a consistent basis. I'll give you some tools to help you incorporate this step into your life in a BALANCED Way™, even if you haven't walked a mile in months.

D — Decide Your Path Forward

At some point, after you've done everything else in a BALANCED Way™, you'll have to just take that leap of faith if you're going to make a change. You'll know when you're ready, and I'll help you get there. Ultimately, right-sizing your career might mean starting your own practice. It might mean foregoing the partner track and working part-time instead. It might even mean leaving the practice of law altogether and finding or creating a whole new career that feels right for you. Whatever you decide, I know it can feel scary, maybe even impossible at times. In this step, I'll share some right-sized lawyer success and life success stories with you, so you know that you're not alone and that it can be done. And I'll give you tools and inspiration to keep you moving closer and closer to your dream come true.

Okay, so grab a pen and a nice notebook that will become your BALANCED Way™ journal. Take a few deep breaths and relax. Here we go!

chapter three
Be True to Yourself

"I prefer to be true to myself, even at the hazard of incurring the ridicule of others, rather than to be false, and to incur my own abhorrence."

FREDERICK DOUGLASS

Your career makeover starts with being true to yourself. That means knowing who you are and being honest about it when identifying your dream job.

Where to Begin

Have you ever taken a career aptitude or personality test? I am a habitual test taker (ahem, a nerd). When I was in college, I kept taking career aptitude tests at the university's Career Counseling Center. Time after time, my results indicated a high aptitude for becoming a teacher, writer, or counselor.

As you've read, I first became a teacher, but of course I'm also a writer and counselor (at law) and more. None of my career decisions were based on the results of the tests I took; at least I didn't think so at the time. It's quite interesting how accurate those tests can be, even though none of them ever pointed to a legal career.

Are Tests Helpful?

They can be. It depends upon how you use them.

As you prepare for your career makeover, tests can be a practical and effective starting point, with a caveat. As Richard L. Bolles says in *What Color Is Your Parachute? 2017* about tests, "I'm not sure how well they'll help you choose a new career," but sometimes they "turn out to be the kind of guidance, the kind of insight, the kind of direction, that career choosers or changers are looking for."

Here are some things to keep in mind when you're taking tests:

- You are unique. There is no person in the world like you, so no test can measure YOU. Tests can only describe a group to which you belong.

- Don't try to figure out ahead of time how you want the test to come out. Stay open to new ideas.

- In taking a test, you should just be looking for clues, hunches, or suggestions, rather than for a definitive answer that tells you what you must do with your life.

- Take several tests and not just one.

- Start with trying to broaden your horizons, and narrow your options down later. Do not try to narrow your options from the outset.

- Know that testing will always have mixed reviews.

So let's jump in and get to know you a little better by way of some tests you might want to try.

Myers-Briggs Type Indicator (MBTI)

One of the best-known personality indicators, the Myers-Briggs Type Indicator (MBTI), was based on Carl Jung's theories on the human psyche. Chances are, you've taken the MBTI before. You might even remember your results. If you've never taken it, or if you have but it's been a while, here's a quick refresher about the MBTI.

The MBTI considers four basic areas of the human psyche, described generally as:

Extroversion/Introversion

Extroverted types learn best by talking and interacting with other people. They process and make sense of new information by interacting with the physical world around them.

Introverted types prefer quiet reflection and privacy. Introverts process information as they explore ideas and concepts internally.

Sensing/Intuition

The second area reflects what people focus their attention on.

Sensing types enjoy a learning environment where the material is presented in a detailed and sequential manner. Sensing types take in what is occurring in the present, and then move on to the abstract after they have established a concrete experience.

Intuitive types prefer a learning environment where the emphasis is placed on meaning and associations. Intuitive types also value insight more than careful observation. Pattern recognition occurs naturally for them.

Thinking/Feeling

The third area reflects a person's decision preferences.

Thinking types search for objective truth and logical principles. They are naturals at deductive reasoning.

Feeling types emphasize issues and causes that can be personalized while they consider other people's motives.

Judging/Perceiving

The fourth area reflects how a person regards complexity.

Judging types will thrive when information is organized and structured, and they will be motivated to complete assignments in order to gain closure. Judging types also like to be on time.

Perceiving types will flourish in a flexible learning environment in which they are stimulated by new and exciting ideas. Perceiving types may be late and/or procrastinate. They tend to actually resist making a decision and dislike closure. (Don't fret if you find that you're a P. The tools in this book will help you overcome that resistance and make the right decision for you, once you have clarity about what that is.)

Should You Take the MBTI?

If you haven't taken the MBTI in a while, or if you've never taken it, I recommend you do so now. Why not? Take a break, grab a cup of coffee or tea, Google "free Myers-Briggs assessment," then take the test and get your own assessment. We'll work on what to do with the results a bit later.

The fun's just beginning.

Got your results? Great. What did you think? Were you surprised? Take a moment to jot down in your BALANCED Way™ journal what stands out for you in terms of reinforcing what you already knew about yourself, as well as any new revelations or ways of thinking about yourself.

For instance, if you're an INFP and hate conflict, you are going to be miserable in a high-conflict position, no matter how much you're being paid. Maybe litigation isn't your thing. As you look at your MBTI results, what other thoughts based on your experiences or interests jump out at you? Jot them down in your journal.

Once you've sat with and considered those results, I recommend you take other tests. Below are some others you might try. Again, when you complete each test, take time to reflect upon the results and jot down thoughts and questions that come to mind.

Enneagram of Personality

The Enneagram of Personality ("Enneagram," for short) is a model of human psyche that categorizes nine different personality types, sometimes called "Enneatypes." According to the Enneagram Institute, the nine basic types by corresponding number are the following:

1: Reformer

Ones are conscientious and ethical, with a strong sense of right and wrong. They are teachers, crusaders, and advocates for change: always striving to improve things, but afraid of making a mistake. Well-organized, orderly, and fastidious, they try to maintain high standards, but can slip into being critical and perfectionistic. They typically have problems with resentment and impatience. At their best, they are wise, discerning, realistic, and noble. They can also be morally heroic.

2: Helper

Twos are empathetic, sincere, and warm-hearted. They are friendly, generous, and self-sacrificing, but can also be sentimental, flattering, and people-pleasing. They are well-meaning and driven to be close to others, but can slip into doing things for others in order to be needed. They typically have problems with possessiveness and with acknowledging their own needs. At their best, they are unselfish and altruistic, and feel unconditional love for others.

3: Achiever

Threes are self-assured, attractive, and charming. Ambitious, competent, and energetic, they can also be status-conscious and highly driven for advancement. They are diplomatic and poised, but can also be overly concerned with their image and what others think of them. They typically have problems with workaholism and competitiveness. At their best, they are self-accepting, authentic, and everything they seem to be – role models who inspire others.

4: Individualist

Fours are self-aware, sensitive, and reserved. They are emotionally honest, creative, and personal, but can also be moody and self-conscious. Withholding themselves from others due to feeling vulnerable and defective, they can also feel disdainful and exempt from ordinary ways of living. They typically have problems with melancholy, self-indulgence, and self-pity. At their best, they are inspired and highly creative, able to renew themselves and transform their experiences.

5: Investigator

Fives are alert, insightful, and curious. They are able to concentrate and focus on developing complex ideas and skills. Independent, innovative, and inventive, they can also become preoccupied with their thoughts and imaginary constructs. They become detached, yet high-strung and intense. They typically have problems with eccentricity, nihilism, and isolation. At their best, they are visionary pioneers, often ahead of their time, and able to see the world in an entirely new way.

6: Loyalist

The committed, security-oriented type, sixes are reliable, hard-working, responsible, and trustworthy. Excellent "troubleshooters," they anticipate problems and foster cooperation, but can also become defensive, evasive, and anxious – running on stress while complaining about it. They can be cautious and indecisive, but also reactive, defiant, and rebellious. They typically have problems with self-doubt and suspicion. At their best, they are internally stable and self-reliant, courageously championing themselves and others.

7: Enthusiast

Sevens are extroverted, optimistic, versatile, and spontaneous. Playful, high-spirited, and practical, they can also misapply their many talents, becoming over-extended, scattered, and undisciplined. They constantly seek new and exciting experiences, but can become distracted and exhausted by staying on the go. They typically have problems with impatience and impulsiveness. At their best, they focus their talents on worthwhile goals, becoming appreciative, joyous, and satisfied.

8: Challenger

Eights are self-confident, strong, and assertive. Protective, resourceful, straight-talking, and decisive, they can also be egocentric and domineering. Eights feel they must control their environment, especially people, sometimes by becoming confrontational and intimidating. Eights typically have problems with their tempers and with allowing themselves to be vulnerable. At their best, they are self-mastering, using their strength to improve others' lives and becoming heroic, magnanimous, and inspiring.

9: Peacemaker

Nines are accepting, trusting, and stable. They are usually creative, optimistic, and supportive, but can also be too willing to go along with others to keep the peace. They want everything to go smoothly and be without conflict, but they can also tend to be complacent, simplifying problems, and minimizing anything upsetting. They typically have problems with inertia and stubbornness. At their best, they are indomitable and all-embracing, able to bring people together and heal conflicts.

The Enneagram of Personality test can be found here: www.enneagraminstitute.com.

The Kolbe® Index

The Kolbe® Index recognizes the concept of a three-part mind with separate domains for thinking, feeling, and doing. The Kolbe® focuses on the conative, or "doing" part of the mind. It contains the instincts that drive a person's natural way of taking action, or their modus operandi (MO).

What are known as Kolbe Action Modes® fall into four basic categories:

- Fact Finder
- Follow Thru
- Quickstart
- Implementor

In addition to assigning a rating for each of the four categories, the Kolbe® also identifies your areas of strength per category. For example, my Kolbe® strength when it comes to Follow Thru is to Systematize. My practice areas of legal life planning (estate planning) and small business representation operate by having systems in place to assist me in following through on projects versus constantly moving on to the next big idea. This helps me keep my Quickstart Action Mode in balance, so that I complete one project before moving on to the next one.

By identifying not only where you are in terms of the Action Modes, but also by identifying your area of strengths within each Action Mode, you can further identify the type of job that aligns with your instincts, and where and how you're most likely to be happy.

The Kolbe A™ Index/Instinct Test costs about $50.00, and you can find it here: www.kolbe.com. Once you have your Kolbe A™ results, you will probably want to learn more about your Career MO, which you can do on the same site.

The Big Five

Maybe it's because I'm such a beach person as well as a canoe enthusiast, but I also love the Big Five test. It assesses your personality in terms of five indicators and is sometimes known as the "OCEAN" test, and sometimes known as the "CANOE" test. They're the same test. It's just that the letters get organized in a different sequence from one acronym to the other. Let's go with "OCEAN."

The indicators are the following:

- Openness to experience

- Conscientiousness

- Extroversion

- Agreeableness

- Neuroticism

Let's say, for example, that you score high in all categories except for Extroversion. If that's the case, you're likely to thrive in a work environment that provides you with a variety of experiences, rather than having too much of the same routine. You'll probably also need your boss and/or co-workers and clients to be likeable, collaborative types who appreciate your attention to detail. Maybe working for a non-profit or serving as a trusted advisor for small, family-owned businesses would suit you.

If you score high in Extroversion and Openness to experience, you might thrive in criminal defense. Obviously, if you score high in Agreeableness, you'll do best in low-conflict positions – whether the conflicts arise from the nature of the practice area or within a particular office setting. These are some examples that come to mind, but take a look at your results, and allow yourself to imagine how they might apply to your current situation or may open you up to imagining a different practice area altogether. You can find this test here: ocean.cambridgeanalytica.org.

One More Test

Another test that I like is the Dewey Color System. It's quick, free, fun to take, and surprisingly accurate in my experience. You can find it here: www.deweycolorsystem.com.

Human Design System

This last recommendation isn't really a test, but you may also want to visit www.jovianarchive.com to learn about the Human Design System and to get your personal Human Design Chart. Human Design offers a map of your unique genetic design, with detailed information on both conscious and unconscious aspects of yourself. One important aspect is to encounter what are called "Signposts of Resistance," which are themes that you risk experiencing when you choose ways of doing things that are not right for you. Human Design tools may help guide you in "discovering your own truth" to find what is right for you as you decide your path forward.

Putting the Information to Use in Your Current Situation

When I was at a small firm in the early years of my practice, I attended a firm retreat. I'd just started at this firm as an associate. As the new kid on the block, I was just getting to know everyone. Towards the end of the day, there was quite a "kumbaya" moment happening. People were hugging and crying, as some had had some fairly profound breakthroughs throughout the day and weekend.

When it was the firm office manager's turn to speak, he announced, "You know, we don't have to like the people we work with. In fact, I don't like most of you, but I still show up every day and do my job."

Awkward moment.

Although surprised by the blunt statement, I felt like this was a legitimate comment from the office manager's perspective. He was the one trying to manage all the petty bickering and back-stabbing that had become a problem. He just wanted everyone to do his or her job and leave him out of the drama.

I was glad he shared his thoughts. After that, I steered clear of him as much as possible because obviously, he wanted to be left alone. And he was one less person that I felt I had to try to win over. There were other, more likeable people that I worked with at that firm who became some of my best friends and mentors, making it a good fit for me overall. If everyone I worked with or my own boss had had an attitude like the office manager's, I probably would not have been as successful or as happy as I was in that position.

Once you are clear on your core values, your instincts, your strengths, weaknesses, and motivators, you can take all that information and use it to your advantage to help identify your dream job. In Chapter 4, we'll talk about how you can take this a step further, so that preferably you can know as much as you can before you accept a new job.

I hope that the tests I've recommended so far have helped you to get to know yourself a little or a lot better, so that you can be honest with yourself about where you are now and where you want to be.

Of course, there are lots and lots of different tests for determining your personality type. I've only touched on a few here, but by now you should be getting to know yourself pretty well.

Look back through the reflections that you jotted down as you considered the results of each test. What patterns do you notice? Are you a person who needs more autonomy than most, or do you thrive by working collaboratively in a group setting? Is having a routine important to you, or is it a total turnoff? How does having a need for security come into play, if at all? What about the need, if any, to connect with people?

I'm sure you noticed that you got a perfect score on each of the tests. The only way to do this wrong is to fail to be true to yourself.

As a person who literally scores off the charts in all categories having to do with nurturing, empathy, and feeling, I was absolutely not the right fit for the corporate job I had. I need a position that puts me in touch with people in a way that helps them solve a problem. So having a corporation as a client, versus people I could connect with on a deeper level, wasn't my ideal situation.

And, no, not all corporate counsel jobs are bad, although that system is often broken. The point is that one size doesn't fit all. Being the lawyer you were born to be means standing out in the crowd and finding the right fit for you instead of conforming to any job or business model that doesn't serve you.

Maybe you, too, need to find your higher calling, and not settle for just a job.

dirk's corner

As Bev stated in the introduction, we wrote this book together, but it's written in the first person as if it was all done by her. Since she's the lawyer, that makes sense. "Dirk's Corner" is a section that provides additional insight from a non-lawyer perspective that may be beneficial to you, as well.

I grew up in the family restaurant business and assumed I'd follow in my father's footsteps. I got through a marketing degree and five years of running a restaurant before realizing that the high stress and long hours weren't worth the money to me. And the money was good. However, flexibility in my schedule and personal time off are more important to me than making the most money possible.

I've always loved travel and adventure, and in 2000, I embarked on a career path as a commercial pilot as a way to incorporate those things into my work life. However, 9/11 happened shortly afterward and changed the aviation industry overnight. A couple of months later, I came across a business idea that seemed tailor-made for me. In addition to loving travel and adventure, I have always been very social and hosted a lot of parties. With the help of my buddy Patrick, party host extraordinaire, I started an online activity-driven outdoor and social club called Adventure Club San Antonio. It is membership-based, and designed as a way for busy professionals to get out and experience more of life while meeting others who share the same interests.

I felt really fortunate to be able to say that I threw parties and took people camping for a living. I ended up running the club for 13 1/2 years before selling it in 2015, just prior to Bev and I embarking on a 14-month around-the-world adventure. The club is how I met Bev, so even if it had never made a dime, it was a smashing success! I'm grateful that I was true to myself and followed my passion, or none of it would have happened.

One of the best ways to be true to yourself is to first determine your core value. Think about what activities make you feel the most blissful. What do you enjoy doing that you can just totally get absorbed in and lose all track of time? Then imagine yourself engaging in that activity in the most ideal situation and conditions you can think of. How does that make you feel? That feeling represents your core value. When facing choices, determine which outcome will move you towards that feeling, and avoid choices that cause you to move further away from that feeling.

Once I determined my core value and moved towards it, I ended up with a really fun business that introduced me to the love of my life. It may not happen for you the same way, but if you aren't true to yourself, you will never know what could have been.

But here's the deal: Being true to yourself can help you be the person you really are; however, that can change as you learn and grow. Don't let that be a reason for inaction, though. It is good to always be open to future possibilities, but don't forget to live in the moment. Don't just be true to yourself; be true to who you are right now. I encourage you to make a list of what you're good at right now, and a separate list of what you're passionate about right now. See where the lists converge.

In 2011, we opened a holistic wellness center in San Antonio. Bev talks more about it in Chapter 7, and there is even more about it in the online Bonus Chapter that you can access by visiting www.happylawyerbonuschapter.com. Before 2010, health and wellness were not on my radar. Being open to new possibilities led me down a different path. Who I was had changed, and to continue being true to myself, my career path changed again, as well. The retail space was only open for a couple of years, but our passion for holistic wellness that sparked its creation lives on in our current endeavors.

There is no magic formula for how to be true to yourself, but hopefully, we've provided some information to help you move in the right direction. One more thing that I'd like to add is to remember you're an original. Stand out. Acknowledge your individuality, and own it. Don't try to live someone else's idea of life. Listen to advice with an open mind, but remember the giver of that advice doesn't know everything about you. Only you do. Advice can provide some great insight, but don't try to squeeze yourself into someone else's mold.

chapter four
Ask and Allow

*"Don't let the noise of others' opinions drown out
your own inner voice. And most important have
the courage to follow your heart and intuition, they
somehow already know what you truly want to become.
Everything else is secondary."*

STEVE JOBS

now that you've got Step 1 of the BALANCED Way™ down, this step will help you ask your inner voice for specific direction that is aligned with your personality type and your true self. Of course, after asking comes allowing. We'll get to that in a bit.

Remember Who You Are

My dad – tall, tough Texan and Naval officer that he was – was known during his lifetime for telling my siblings and me, "Remember who you are." When we were growing up, he emphasized it every time we walked out the door to go on a date or to a party, followed by, "and make me proud." You didn't mess with my no-nonsense dad, and his legacy lives on. His mantra has been passed down to his grandchildren and great-grandchildren.

Now that I'm getting older and hopefully wiser myself, I like to think of Dad's words in a spiritual sense.

"Remember who you are" has especially resonated with me since his passing in 2005. I think of Dad, feel his presence, and still hear his counsel daily. He is and always has been my favorite angel.

But what does "Remember who you are" mean, exactly?

Dad was pragmatic and held us to high standards of behavior, so I know when he used that phrase, he meant, "Don't do anything stupid that will end up being an embarrassment to yourself or your family." He did not intend it to be a philosophical statement. But I have more metaphysical leanings and tend to take things in that direction, so stay with me. I believe this will serve you well in your career transition, too.

In the last chapter, I presented you with practical tools to help you begin to identify the type of practice and office setting that might be right for you. I realize the prospect of making those changes you may be contemplating can feel burdensome, scary, or even impossible.

This step takes that practical information to a spiritual level so that you can also approach your career transition soulfully. This is where you learn to identify what feels right for you; what your true calling is.

I mentioned earlier that one of my favorite books is *Ask and It Is Given*. In it, the channeled entity known as Abraham says that, even before you were born, you knew who you were. "You came forth into this wonderful body, remembering the joyous, powerful nature that is you, knowing that you would always remember the splendor of the Source from which you came, knowing that you could never lose your connection with that Source."

Because you cannot separate yourself from Source (which I call God), and because God is a beneficent God who loves you and wants you to be, do, and have all that you desire, ergo, there is nothing that you cannot be, do, or have.

I know, I know. I can hear you saying, "No, Bev. That's not how it works. I can't pray real hard, and suddenly find myself lying in a hammock in Tahiti with all of my bills paid, everyone in my family healthy, and no cares in the world."

I get it. That's exactly how I felt just before my own shift happened.

A Pivotal, "Deep Prayer" Moment

It happened back in October of 2007. Dirk and I were in our second year of marriage. I was bored with my law job, but it had always paid the bills and I was with a good firm, so I kept at it. In the middle of one particularly hectic week, I did the unthinkable. I left work early and took the next day off, knowing that my deadlines would still be there when we returned and a little freaked out about how I'd get it all done. But I have a 100% track record of getting it all done, so we loaded up our wonder dog Pups and a few supplies, and we drove off into the night.

We headed down south to our favorite beach camping spot along the Texas coast known as Big Shell. It's very remote, and you need a 4WD vehicle to get there. At certain times of the year, you can camp down there for days and only see a few trucks and park rangers pass by. That was the case this time.

That night, we sat in Dirk's Jeep Cherokee to avoid the high coastal winds and have a serious talk about a lot of crazy things that had started happening in our lives. I suddenly entered into an involuntary trance state. What I mean by that is, I wasn't intentionally moving, but my arms began to move very, very slowly. I lost most of my ability to speak for a few minutes or so, and my body shook. It was more like light convulsions, actually. My lips trembled.

This was the first time in my life that I had a witness to what I had always considered one of my "deep prayer" moments. I was about to receive a very important message from God. I knew it because this is the way it had always happened. "I should really pray more," I would always think afterwards. "God loves me." The messages always came through with such clarity.

That night, although my speech when it returned was labored and slow, I finally managed to ask Dirk, "Do. You. See. What. I. Am. Doing?" "Does. This. Happen. To. You?" He stared at me, while my right arm moved – ever so painstakingly and still without my control – as if I was fastening my seat belt.

Dirk replied, "No."

Oh.

Pups was oblivious as he slept on my lap.

I'd wondered for years, but had never asked anyone, whether their "deep prayer" looked like my "deep prayer." I found it a little odd that no one ever talked about it, but I never had any reason to bring it up to anyone. It seemed so private and personal. And to me, it seemed normal.

That night was the beginning of a huge shift in my life. Although it still took years, I began to understand and embrace my ability to "find my own north star," as best-selling author and life coach Martha Beck calls it in her book that is appropriately titled *Finding Your Own North Star*. I learned to trust my intuition because I knew it was divinely inspired. This was an epiphany, discovering that the answers I had been in search of for years were within me and would reveal themselves if I stopped resisting and started allowing.

Bringing this all back to Dad's mantra, I believe that part of us always remembers who we are and what we came here to do, who we came here to be. We can ask for guidance and allow the answers we need to flow toward us.

(BTW, the message I received, among several others that night, was, "Fasten your seatbelt." If you enjoy reading about paranormal experiences and want to know what else happened that night, as well as some amazing things since then, visit www.happylawyerbonuschapter.com to access the Bonus Chapter of this book. Dirk wrote all of that one, and he'll be delighted to share it with you.)

Truly Divine Inspiration

I also believe that *everyone*, including you, has the ability to tap into his or her own intuition and ask for guidance. Whether through prayer, meditation, or whatever name you give your asking, you can ask, and you will be answered. It's a gift we all have, and I'd even say it's our birthright, although it will manifest differently and to varying degrees from one person to another.

Your experiences won't look or feel exactly like mine, and that's a good thing. You're an original, after all! If you want to have your own divine experience, you can. I hope you choose to give it a go, but it's up to you. As I told you in Chapter 1, here you're in charge.

You start by dropping the resistance and being open to the guidance when it comes. My torts professor in law school, Professor Ferguson, used to drill into our heads: "Don't fight the facts." It's a lot like that.

You have to stop resisting (stop "fighting the facts") and allow things to flow. As Martha Beck states in *Finding Your Own North Star*, "The more closely [people] follow their physical and emotional 'compasses,' the more they begin to sense intuitive guidance. As they draw closer and closer to living in harmony with their essential selves, they often begin to report wildly improbable coincidences, strong impressions of distant events, or a sense of knowing certain things about their own future."

This is so true. Stay open.

When Dirk and I had our holistic wellness center that I mentioned at the end of Chapter 3, word got out about my intuitive talents. (Yeah, thanks, Dirk.) I was asked on several occasions to consult about issues relating to health and wellness, career transformations, and more. What I found, time after time, is that people who were open to intuitive experiences began to have profound "coincidences" and encounters in their lives after a session with me. To be sure, they also always felt a new sense of peace and calming that usually had eluded them up to the time of our session. I was happy to play some part in their shift.

But I want to make this clear: I don't believe they needed me to have many of these connections. However, I will acknowledge that it probably made it easier for the person seeking the guidance to "feel" the message, to hear the message, and to trust the message when they sat with me. It felt more real to them that way, which allowed them to stay open, get out of their own way, and allow things to flow.

So how can you do this on your own?

If you haven't read *Ask and It Is Given* yet, I highly recommend you make it a part of your career transition plan. As Abraham so eloquently explains throughout the book, you do create your own reality. In the book are 22 processes to help you identify and get more of what you want. While I recommend you have fun with each of those 22 processes, we won't go into all of them here. For purposes of this book, here are a few strategies I recommend to help you get used to asking and allowing.

First, whatever your slow-down vibe is, do it often. Do you prefer meditation, channeling, prayer; do you consider all of those to be the same thing, or are they separate things and you do them at different times for different reasons? What's the language that you use to refer to getting quiet, being still, and just listening to your inner voice? Whatever term or practice you use, whenever you use it, make a date with yourself to do that daily.

Yes, I said daily. You can do this!

Meditation

If you're just getting started with meditation, I recommend you check out a book called *The Anxious Lawyer: An 8-Week Guide to a Happier, Saner Law Practice Using Meditation*, by lawyers Jeena Cho and Karen Gifford. It's an excellent read. You can also email us at info@balanced-way.com for additional recommendations. Or you can just find a quiet, comfortable place and give it a go on your own.

Here's how:

Set your timer. You can start with as few as five minutes and build up from there as you train your mind to be still.

Sit in a relaxed position.

Keep your back, neck, and head vertically aligned. Relax your shoulders.

Bring your attention to your breathing, and observe your breath as it flows in and out. Give that feeling your full attention. When your attention drifts, which is normal, note it, let it go, and gently bring your attention back to your breathing.

Don't get frustrated or give up if you find it challenging to be still at first. That's normal. Consistency is the key, so stay with it.

Ask to receive clarity on what you need to know to take the next step. Listen for the answer, but also know that it might not come immediately. Don't try to force it. Be easy and light-hearted about it.

Get Outside

We're going to cover exercise in greater detail in Chapter 9, but it deserves a mention here, too. Get outside. Take walks. Listen to the songbirds. If you live near the beach, walk there and listen to the sound of the waves. If you live near the woods, take a walk there and listen to the sound of the trees blowing in the wind. Did I mention, breathe…?

Journaling/Morning Pages

In her best-selling book called *The Artist's Way*, author Julia Cameron recommends doing what she calls "morning pages." The idea is to journal three pages every morning, with no other purpose necessarily than to get your thoughts out of your head. I also recommend making morning pages a part of your BALANCED Way™ journal, no matter what time of day you actually do them.

How do you do them? As Cameron says, "There is no wrong way to do morning pages." Your morning pages don't have to sound smart or artistic. Again, the idea is to just write three pages of whatever uncensored thoughts enter your mind. Anyone can do this. When I taught middle school English, even my reluctant writers came to love our free-writing time.

If you find that you can't think of anything to write, just start writing what you're grateful for. Surely, you can fill up three pages about that: a roof over your head, a comfortable bed, the hot cup of coffee you are drinking while you're writing, a loving family, healthy children, the fact that you have a job that allows you to pay your bills, which is more than a lot of people can say, etc. Keep going. Also, write whatever else comes to you, just three pages, unless you want to write more. Do this every day, and don't hold back or pre-judge what you're going to write before you write it. When you consistently do your morning pages, you'll discover how powerful this exercise is, especially when you combine it with daily meditation.

Some other things you might consider writing about in your morning pages or meditating about are:

- What would you do if money were no object?

- How much do you really need vs. how much do you need just so you can look the part?

- What do you need to know about your relationship with money and how can you find out?

- How are you meant to serve?

- Who are you meant to work with?

- What's the best way to put to use the information you've learned so far?

- What would you do if you weren't afraid? (Which brings me to recommend another of my favorite books: the classic *Who Moved My Cheese? An Amazing Way to Deal with Change in Your Work and in Your Life*. It's a quick little motivational fable that you might want to read or re-read.)

- Start your own practice?

- Learn a new area of practice?

- Work part-time and/or from home or other non-traditional location?

- Move to a different city, state or country?

- Learn a new skill, so you can leave the practice of law altogether, either temporarily or permanently?

Be open to exploring these ideas and other new ideas. You don't have to take action on any of it that doesn't feel right, but keep asking and allowing answers, experiences, ideas, and people to come into your life.

Vision Board

I love doing vision boards for lots of reasons, including the fact that they're easy for a not-so-crafty girl like me, plus the materials are readily available and cost almost nothing.

You need:

- Poster board
- Glue
- A big stack of magazines or pics that have been downloaded off the Internet and printed out. (Hint: magazines are more fun.)
- Soft, lyric-free music. Music with lyrics will become distracting, and you want to give your full attention to your vision board.
- Optional: fancy pens and/or stickers

There are a variety of ways to do vision boards, but ultimately the idea is to jump in and do it. You can't do it wrong, as long as you're having fun with it and creating boards that inspire you. Clip words and photos that represent the life you want to have and paste them onto the board. You can even do this on your phone or computer with Pinterest, but I'm a real paper and scissors gal, personally.

Invite your friends over and do this as a group activity, attend a vision board workshop, or go it alone if that's what you're feeling. Either way, the point is to have fun with it!

I know, I know … "But Bev! I don't have time for all this stuff! I hit the ground running when my alarm clock goes off every day, and I collapse in my bed at night, exhausted."

I understand. I promise I've been there, and some days I feel like I still am. Ultimately, this is about finding what works for you. Maybe you'll find that you're able to meditate in the morning, get outside at lunch, journal while you're at your kid's karate class, and squeeze in some of the other activities on weekends. Maybe you'll find that it works best to have lunch alone some days, so you can journal instead of participating in the usual gossip sessions or power lunches. When I had my corporate counsel job, I often journaled and meditated during my lunch break, which I became increasingly, fiercely protective of.

If you deem it important, you'll find a way. Nothing about this step should feel stressful. Again, be easy about it.

This is about relaxing, enjoying, tuning in, and being mindful. As glimpses into what could be your new life reveal themselves to you in moments at a time, keep asking and allowing, keep saying thank you, revel in the joy of being you, and keep up the good work.

As you come into contact with people, articles, books, and information and have that "perfect timing" or "in sync" feeling, jot down these experiences and your feelings about them in your journal, too.

Remain open to learning about job leads or other career moves from unexpected sources. Dig deeper and check in with your inner voice as you explore these new ideas.

You'll get better and better at knowing what questions to ask as you work through this process. *You'll* know what's right for *you*.

In the words of insightful Abraham:

"Others are often eager to guide you. There are endless people – with endless opinions, rules, requirements, and suggestions for how you should live your life, but none of them are able to take into consideration the only thing that matters in achieving your desires: Others cannot understand the vibrational content of your desires, and they cannot understand the vibrational content of where you are, so they are not in any way equipped to guide you. Even when they have the very best of intentions and want your absolute Well-Being, they do not know. And even though many of them attempt to be unselfish, it is never possible for them to separate their desire for you from their own desire for themselves."

Trust your own inner voice. It will remind you who you are and will guide you to becoming the lawyer and the person you were meant to be.

dirk's corner

When that experience on the beach that Bev described above happened, it felt like a whole new world opening up to me. I didn't even know what was really happening at the time. By then I had known Bev for about four and a half years, and knew her well enough to know that she wasn't faking it. She never likes to be the center of attention or create controversy, and outing herself as an intuitive in this book is not easy for her.

I don't experience the same thing she does, but I have learned to look inward for answers sometimes, instead of just outward. Our intuition and great ideas that come from "out of nowhere" don't really come from out of nowhere. Since that time on the beach, I have been able to recognize when that happens and appreciate it.

In the years that have passed, we have learned a lot from Bev's ability to connect in that way. It's great, because we never feel like we are alone when facing decisions. One of the most important things we have learned is how our thoughts create our reality. Everything that exists consists of pure energy, at its most basic level, that resonates at various frequencies. These differences in frequency are what make one thing different from another. When we think about something, we are working towards creating that reality for ourselves by emitting a certain frequency. It's like we send out a beacon to draw in whatever we are thinking. It's called manifestation, and is a powerful unseen force. I encourage you to tap into it, and magical things could happen for you. Thoughts are things. When you think about something you want in your life, think about it from the position of being grateful that you already have it, instead of from a position of wanting it in the future.

To help you develop your intuitive side, you might consider joining a Meetup.com group or other organization geared toward intuitive and spiritual activities, or consider working with an intuitive coach to help enhance and develop your natural intuitive talents.

As Bev says, even if you don't think you have intuitive abilities, you do, to at least some degree. You'll discover them, and they will serve you well, if you set the intention and stay open.

chapter five

Let Go of What No Longer Serves You

"All the art of living lies in a fine mingling
of letting go and holding on."

HAVELOCK ELLIS

i have to warn you. One of the uncomfortable things that will happen as you go through the BALANCED Way™ program and get closer and closer to becoming the lawyer you were meant to be is that you will have a lower tolerance for things that no longer serve you. You'll find yourself needing to decide what to hold onto and what to let go of. But that's a good thing.

There's no better time than now to take mental inventory of what you're dragging around that no longer serves you, your family, or your highest purpose.

Take Your Pack Off

During 2015-2016, Dirk and I were really fortunate to get to do a 14-month, around-the-world trip (our "RTW"). For over a year, we researched everything there is to know about what we should pack. We knew we'd need to bring camping gear so we could attend festivals and get off the beaten path when we wanted to. The camping gear took up a lot of room in our packs.

At our age, we knew we didn't really want to look like backpackers everywhere we went for over a year, so we needed to pack one nice outfit and proper shoes for going out. And even though we were chasing summer, summer everywhere in the world doesn't feel like summer in South Texas; so, we needed to be prepared with cold-weather (for us) clothing and rain gear. We also needed hiking boots. And our electronics. Oh yeah, and funky garb to wear at the festivals. And our essential oils. And a water purifying kit. And our water flasks and nutritional supplements.

I needed my journals because we only had one laptop, so I preferred to write out my journal entries that, ideally, would turn into blog posts. We were always behind on the blog, so I carried several journals at the same time. Sometimes we also carried travel books that were lent to us and related to the particular country or continent we were visiting at that time. (If you want to know what else we packed and/or what gear we recommend, check out our travel blog at www.EarthBurners.com. We still make periodic posts.)

We went through our packs and mailed things home to ourselves from Spain, Denmark, Greece, and the Philippines. We carried some things home during a planned five-day layover in Texas when we were traveling from New Zealand to Colombia, and we sent some items home with our friend Scott, who met up with us in South Africa.

Now, understand that we weren't really backpacking as you probably are thinking of that term. We stayed in some really nice Airbnbs, were invited to stay with host families in some beautiful homes, and had private rooms even when we stayed in hostels. But still. We walked a lot of miles from train stations to our accommodations and many other points from A to B carrying those packs.

Even though we frequently sent packages home, our backpacks were still always too heavy. I blame our unexpected and unfortunate early return home, due to Dirk's torn meniscus, partially on those heavy packs.

Why did we do it to ourselves?

Because, priorities.

Just like I said in the last chapter, you will always create space for what you choose to have in your life. In my case, that included a flat iron, a variety of shoes, and several journals that I lugged around the world.

I'll tell you what, though. Carrying extra weight in the physical, literal sense can be a lot easier than doing it in the figurative sense.

This step is about learning to take the proverbial pack off and rest a while, another piece of sage advice from my Daddy. He told me that often; I just didn't listen for a long time. Once you do that, after you sit down and breathe, you've got to go through that pack and decide what is worth keeping and what may be stopping you from having the life you dream of.

Get out your BALANCED Way™ journal, and get ready to start brainstorming what you might be dragging around in your life that no longer serves you. What's been stopping you from having what you want?

Here are some ideas that I came up with.

- Worrying about what people think of you
- Having to be right, perfect, better, smarter, or richer
- Looking only within the legal community for answers to your questions
- The belief that you are stuck
- Willingness to participate in toxic relationships
- Maintaining a certain lifestyle that's making you miserable
- The belief that no one appreciates you anyway, so why does it matter?
- The exhaustion that comes from doing everything for your kids (or your spouse)
- The belief that you're not enough

- A conviction that life is hard

- The resignation that you're not supposed to feel good after age 40, or 50, or whatever other age you've resigned yourself to

- An unhealthy lifestyle that is keeping you from living life to its fullest

- Do any of these resonate with you?

Write down in your journal each of the above beliefs that is present in your life.

When you're done, I want you to add to the list. Write down any additional limiting beliefs that are present in your life besides the ones I've suggested. Take your time. Maybe you can only come up with two or three more at first, but I'll bet that once you get going, you can come up with a pretty long list. Be honest with yourself.

When you've done that, go through the list and jot down three facts that support each limiting belief you wrote down. For example, if you wrote down a conviction that life is hard, maybe your three supporting facts are: "1) My teenager keeps getting into trouble at school; 2) my legal assistant is incompetent, but my caseload is too full to take the time to find a replacement; and 3) my mom was recently diagnosed with cancer." Go ahead and write down your facts evidencing why each of those things on your list is true.

Next, go through your list and turn each of the limiting beliefs into a positive statement. For example, if you wrote down that you worry too much about what people think of you, I want you to turn that statement around to something like: "I am not concerned about others' opinions of me." Go through your entire list and turn all of those limiting beliefs into beliefs that align with the person you want to become.

You see where this is headed, I'm sure. Now I want you to go through each of the positivåe statements on your list and come up with three facts in your life that support each of the new statements. For example, if you turned the last bullet point around by writing, "My healthy lifestyle allows me to do everything I want to do in my life," now you're going to write three (or more, if you want) reasons why that's true or could be true. Things like, "1) I exercise for at least 30 minutes, five days out of the week ..." and so on.

Once you've got three factual statements for each positive statement, I encourage you to add more. I hope you'll start to see that you are already well on your way to becoming the lawyer and the person you want to be. What might have felt insurmountable and impossible actually has a chance of success, depending upon your priorities and what you choose to keep in your proverbial pack.

You can always find a thought that feels better than the one you have; and I'd argue that you can always substantiate that better-feeling-thought or find a way that it could be substantiated if you wanted to.

Here's the kicker: You can always choose to keep things that you know no longer serve your highest purpose. It's your choice.

Let me give you a few examples of what can happen when you start to let go of what no longer serves you and replace it with something that does.

Worrying About What Other People Think of You

My empathic ways almost didn't allow me to add this one to the list because obviously we have to care what people think of us to some degree in order to maintain healthy relationships. Otherwise, it would always just be all about you, and who would that serve? So I think "Don't worry what others think" can sometimes be a dangerous statement to get too carried away with. It can easily lead to, "Screw you. I'm going to do what I want regardless of how it affects you."

Having said that, I've been that person who worries to an extreme degree what others think. I'd spend 15 minutes writing a one-sentence post on Facebook, and then I'd still edit it. In fact, the running joke between Dirk and me used to be that all of my comments on Facebook would show up as "edited." Every single one. As I said, I'm an empath. I didn't want to offend anyone by having them read my comments the wrong way. Thank God, I've gotten over that. Mostly.

And the reason I was finally able (mostly) to get over it is because I realized that my playing small, my making sure everyone is okay with what I think, how I look, what I'm doing, and on and on, wasn't serving anyone. It wasn't making me or my loved ones happy. Worse than that, it was keeping me from doing what I came here to do. You can't start a movement when you're worried about every little post on social media.

I also realized the very important truism that is, not that many people are actually looking anyway. Most people aren't paying that much attention because they are busy worrying about what I think about them.

So I chose to stand out and be noticed.

If that's an issue for you, you've got to let it go, no matter how comfortable it's been. There's a new topic for your meditation or morning pages. You didn't come here to play small and to allow fear of what others think to stop you from becoming the lawyer and the person you were born to be, either.

Let's move on to another limiting belief.

Having to Be Right, Perfect, Better, Smarter, or Richer

How many of these have you tried to be? Uh-oh. You, too? There's something about us lawyers, whether it's our training or what caused us to seek out this profession in the first place, where we just have to be right. Okay, obviously I'm not the first person who has noticed that, but did you know you can lose the part of that urge that doesn't serve you? I mean, it's one thing to zealously represent your client and all that entails; it's quite another to argue with everyone about everything and always have to have the last word.

Oh, my. I never knew I did this until I finally started really listening to myself as a result of some belief work that I did with a fellow holistic practitioner named Brenda Bailey. Brenda owns a company called Unlimited Possibilities 101 and – among her many talents – is a ThetaHealing® Master. ThetaHealing® is a technique that focuses on thought and prayer, teaches you how to put to use your natural intuition, and helps you replace beliefs that no longer serve you with more positive beliefs that do. When I first started doing ThetaHealing®, I was really surprised at the lengths I'd go to be right about the smallest thing. I'd do it nicely most of the time because my mom raised me, but I was still right, you know.

If this is you, you can choose to ditch that, and I hope you do. It's annoying, and it doesn't serve anyone. Just keep the part of the urge that motivates you to prevail in a contested case or something else that actually matters to someone, and go get 'em!

Looking Only Within the Legal Community for Answers to Your Questions

This is a heretical thought. During your career transition, have you considered looking outside the legal community for the problem you're trying to solve?

Let me give you an example of what I mean. Alexis Neely, whom I am honored to have written the foreword for this book, already had a successful practice of her own when she started looking outside of the legal community to learn how she could improve her law business. She started looking at how other businesses were run. What resulted is not just a thriving business, which you'll read more about in Chapter 10, but she has started a movement.

She figured out that the same old way of practicing law, the standard way of billing clients and the same old way of how many lawyers "serve" their clients without putting them first, was not the right fit for her firm. The standard model was preventing her from serving her clients in the way she was meant to serve. In a nutshell, the one-size-fits-all mindset had to go. Now her clients love her, and she loves her clients and her business.

Now let's look at an example of what can happen when you choose to do things the same old way you've always done them.

An Unhealthy Lifestyle that Is Keeping You from Living Life to Its Fullest

Ted, a family friend of Dirk's, is a good example of this. Ted had a thriving law practice for years. In addition to being what his colleagues considered a good lawyer, Ted had a good business acumen. Along with his financial success came what many would call "the finer things in life." Ted appeared to have it all: big house as well as a comfortable vacation home, nice cars, good looks, great career, beautiful and loving family. Ted lived large.

Unfortunately, Ted was also a smoker and a meat-and-potatoes kind of guy. He never made it a point to exercise and would circle the parking lot waiting for a "rock star" parking space to open up, so he could avoid having to walk an extra hundred feet. He was a heavy drinker of vodka, and was known to keep secret bottles stashed at friends' homes so he could indulge without his wife knowing. In short, Ted seemingly never gave one thought to how his daily decisions were affecting his health. He was the kind of person who had the attitude, "I've only got one life, and I'm going to live it." To his credit, he certainly seemed to, on his terms.

Ted's business did so well, he was all set to enjoy the fruits of his labors and retire well before he grew "old." Sadly, thirteen days after Ted retired, he had a heart attack and died. He was 54.

The choices we make on a daily basis regarding our physical health have a direct result on our ability to live our lives to the fullest. They also have a direct result on what happens to our families.

If you think your lifestyle might be preventing you from living life for the amount of time you'd like to stick around and be a part of your family, then you are probably right.

You are not alone. This is the elephant in the room that so many lawyers don't talk about. Too often, we're busy looking the part, posting photos of ourselves with a cigar, an extravagant meal, and a well-deserved cocktail after a big win and/or a hard week at the office.

Hey, I'm all for celebrating and unwinding. Don't get me wrong. I just want you to ask yourself whether your overall lifestyle supports your dream come true or hinders it. If it hinders it, you can change that. I hope you choose to.

In the next few chapters, we're going to dig deeper into why it's critical to maintain your physical health – not only during your career transition, but also throughout your legal career. Because lawyering is thought of as a "desk job," and rightfully so, there's a tendency to ignore the effect that poor physical health can and does have on any lawyer's career.

I'm on a mission to change that. I not only want to create happy lawyers; I want to create healthy lawyers. Because honestly, the two go hand in hand. More on that later.

Take Inventory of What's in Your Pack

For now, here's what I'd like for you to do: take some time to look back through the beliefs and supporting facts that you've written down in your journal. For each of those limiting beliefs that no longer serves you, no matter how many supporting facts you have that make each one true, I want you to acknowledge the place that that belief has had in your life. It has served a purpose, whether you deem it good or bad, and it has helped to create the person you are today. Take a moment or a few to reflect upon it if you need to, then – when you feel ready – let it go. It might not happen all in one day or even one month; it will likely require prayer, meditation, journaling, and whatever else you can do to slow down and listen to your inner voice. But eventually, I hope you will choose to do this for each limiting belief you wrote down.

I also encourage you to repeat this exercise every time your negative thoughts and emotions feel like they're getting the best of you.

The most important part of the exercise is to then turn your attention to all those positive beliefs and supporting facts that you also wrote down. Start repeating these statements to yourself, over and over, and incorporate the concepts into your vision board, journaling, conversations, actions, and life in general.

Notice how light your "pack" is starting to feel, and be vigilant about not putting back in the things that you know no longer serve you.

Congratulations! You are well on your way to having the career and life of your dreams!

dirk's corner

Admittedly, this one has been tough for Bev and me. But don't be afraid to let go of friendships or relationships that pull you down instead of raising you up. If you cringe when you see a particular person calling or texting you, and only respond out of feeling obligated or because you've known them for a long time, it may be time to let that relationship fade.

Shortly after we returned from our RTW, Bev saw the name of someone we'd known for a few years pop up on an incoming call. She let it go to voicemail, and agonized over the thought of calling back. The person is a nice enough person, but is also one of those energy vampires who is constantly running in circles. Past conversations with that person left Bev exhausted and drained. The voicemail indicated this time would be no different. I suggested to Bev to just not call back this time and delete that phone contact. She agonized even more over that idea, but she did it.

Work on building relationships with people who bring out the best in you and inspire you, instead of bringing you down. It's easy to get stuck with only what's familiar. Brilliant thinkers come from all walks of life. You may find answers in places that surprise you.

The next time you're contemplating doing something and the thought *what will people think?* pops into your head, say to yourself *I refuse to live in the prison of what other people think.*

chapter six
Alkalize to Optimize

"In my later years, I have looked in the mirror each day and found a happy person staring back. Occasionally I wonder why I can be so happy. The answer is that every day of my life I've worked only for myself and for the joy that comes from writing and creating. The image in my mirror is not optimistic, but the result of optimal behavior."

RAY BRADBURY

this step is all about optimizing you. That means, among other things, learning to value your health as one of your greatest assets and having the amount of energy you need to take on the demands of your career makeover and more.

I mentioned the elephant in the room in the last chapter: lawyering is all too often a very unhealthy profession. Thankfully, there is more awareness of this when it comes to mental health, stress, substance abuse, depression, and suicide. There seems to be an increased interest in addressing the problem, but our profession has a long way to go.

A study entitled "The Prevalence of Substance Use and Other Mental Health Concerns Among American Attorneys" that was reported in the *Journal of Addiction Medicine* in 2016 found that lawyers are drinking too much, struggling with substance abuse, and suffering from depression, anxiety, and stress.

Sadly, we know this is nothing new. A higher prevalence of suicide, alcohol/drug abuse, depression, stress, and anxiety among lawyers when compared to other professionals, including doctors, has been known for decades. However, the shame and fear of being ostracized for speaking up about these problems persist among our profession.

I'm thankful that more is being done, finally, to address these issues; and I'm happy if my telling my story is one drop in a large bucket of work that still needs to done. As more and more big firms move in the direction of providing health and wellness related programs, as well as educational resources for their employees, let us not forget though that part of that big elephant in the room is the average lawyer's less than optimum physical health, and not just their mental health. Personally, I believe you can't have one without the other.

As lawyer and co-author of *The Anxious Lawyer: An 8-Week Guide to a Happier, Saner Law Practice Using Meditation,* Jeena Cho advises, "Value your own well-being and the well-being of your workforce. Your own health – physical, emotional, and psychological health – is one of your most important assets.

This requires consistent effort and attention. Stressful times are inevitable in law practice, but our mind and body can only handle so much chronic stress before getting ill."

I couldn't agree more.

That's why these next few chapters focus on ways to help you make sure you're at the top of your game, physically and mentally. I had to learn the hard way that going from one greener pasture to the next in a never-ending quest for the perfect law job was never going to be *the* answer. Like you undoubtedly, I had to be mentally and physically capable, day after day, to meet the demands of the legal profession: grabbing a quick bite of whatever was easy while working long hours to get that brief filed on time; attending client meetings, court hearings, and/or mediations that ran late into the evening; lugging who-knows-how-many pounds of bankers boxes full of documents around; trying to stay awake during yet another very dry and tedious deposition; and so many other physical challenges that no one told me about in law school.

Look, I'm not saying this is the most physically or even mentally demanding profession in the world. I'm just suggesting that being prepared to meet the demands that *do* exist goes a long way towards being the lawyer you were meant to be.

In my health journey, the first thing I learned about that really made a difference for me was the concept of maintaining an alkaline diet. I know it sounds too simple, but allow me to share my story with you.

A Little Background About My Own Health Journey

Like a lot of lawyers, I was both sick and healthy for years.

When I was in my second year of law school, two weeks after my second son was born, I came down with a life-threatening bacterial infection called shigella. That was a rough time, but obviously – thank God – I survived it.

For 15 years after that, my digestive system just never felt right. I am not a doctor, so I don't know if it was related to the infection or just a bad coincidence, but I was plagued with "tummy problems" for years. My dad suffered from Crohn's disease, and I knew it was important to watch what I ate and follow all the standard advice about diet. I didn't know back then that I was falling far short of feeling as good as I could feel. I just thought I would always feel like I did.

Like most people I know, I thought I maintained a pretty healthy diet, but – not knowing any more than I knew – I was still following the Standard American Diet ("S.A.D."), thinking, "Everything in moderation." Among other practices I knew were not healthy without realizing how destructive they were, I loved my diet soda.

I started drinking it in college, but I didn't become an addict until law school. Thankfully, I didn't drink it during pregnancy or when I was still nursing, but I never thought about the fact that I wasn't any more tired – even during pregnancy and the post-partum months – without my diet soda as I was when I continued to drink it.

When I was studying for the bar exam, I read that it was better to give up caffeine altogether and drink lots of water to stave off the fatigue that sets in when the caffeine wears off. That made sense, so I tried it. It worked, and I made it through the physical demands of studying for and taking the bar exam. Hurray! But once I got licensed and started practicing law, I still went back to my diet soda and my coffee. For years, this is pretty much all I drank other than an occasional glass of wine or iced tea.

Sound familiar?

As I mentioned before, for many years I also suffered from depression and from severe chronic fatigue. Since lawyers tend not to talk about that elephant in the room, I thought it was just me. I had no idea how prevalent these conditions are in our profession. Since that time, I've told people that I was the healthiest sickly person around, or the sickest healthy person, depending on how you look at it.

Somehow I managed to keep all the plates spinning, but I certainly was not thriving. I got to the point where it was not unusual for me to fall asleep on the highway while driving home from work or a late board meeting. It was scary! I would sometimes call Dirk to talk to me while driving so I wouldn't doze off.

Again, I didn't corner the market on lawyers being stressed out, burned out, and exhausted. I feel pretty sure you can relate to a lot of this or know a lawyer who can. But it doesn't have to be that way.

I've Come a Long Way

I can't tell you that I have any special elixir or methods to cure what might ail you. As I said, I am not a medical doctor, but I am a certified nutrition coach, blood microscopist, essential oils junkie, and a few other health-nut things, in addition to being a pretty smart lawyer.

As I'll talk more about in the next chapter, I did a lot of research and became my own guinea pig, so to speak. I knew I had to change something, and I read that alkalinity could be part of the solution. I had nothing to lose by giving it a try. That was a defining moment in my life. I honestly did not expect it to work as well as it did, but I felt like I was starting to get some energy back.

I kept at it, while also incorporating other things into my life that made such a huge difference in my ability to lawyer, with confidence, and without wanting to punch a hole in the wall.

So here it is years later, and Dirk and I still stick with this same program that I'm about to reveal to you, and we still recommend it to anyone who asks. And we're glad that folks *have* asked because those who have actually followed the program have reported the same or similar positive experiences that he and I have had. Like us, some people have experienced some really profound, life-changing results.

Why Alkalinity Matters

Your blood must stay at a pH of or very near 7.365, which is slightly alkaline. Your body will do what it has to in order to keep it there, even if it has to leach alkaline minerals from your bones and organs to counteract acidity.

A 2012 review published in the *Journal of Environmental and Public Health* found that balancing your body's pH through an alkaline diet can be helpful in reducing morbidity and mortality from numerous chronic diseases and ailments. I'm all for that, aren't you? As I already mentioned was the case for me, it can also lead to much higher energy levels. Unfortunately, most of the typical Western diet is highly acidic, and that's a problem that few people talk about or are aware of.

It's not that hard to fix this, though, by drinking alkaline water and eating alkaline-forming foods.

Alkaline Water

So first, let's talk about the water. If you're like the overwhelming majority of the world's population and don't have access to your own, natural, alkaline water source, here are some ways to get alkaline water.

You can buy bottled alkaline water.

You can buy bottled alkaline water, but I don't recommend it if you have any other choice among those listed in this chapter.

It's only included on this list because it's become so popular, and we're often asked about it.

When you add it all up, purchasing enough bottled water to keep yourself and your family properly hydrated for years on end is the most expensive choice you can make when it comes to drinking alkaline water. It's also the least healthy option, and that's not optimizing anything except for profits of the bottled water industry. The only time Dirk and I drink bottled water is when we're traveling and don't have easy access to better options.

Most bottled waters are acidic, but even those that we've tested that are labeled as alkaline are still oxidizing, which is not good. And we've tested dozens of bottled waters, including those that you are most likely familiar with. Pretty much every plastic bottle of water on a store shelf contains chemical residues from the plastic, not to mention the environmental impact of having to bottle that water and transport it. Yuck.

If you love your brand of bottled water and are convinced that it's healthy and safe to drink, I hope you'll do your own research, including watching *For Love of Water (F.L.O.W.)* and *Tapped*. Visit www.happylawyerbook.com to access our A-Z Wellness Guide, which includes information about healthy drinking water.

You can add lemon juice or lemon essential oil to your water.

Another thing you can do to alkalize your drinking water is to squeeze some fresh lemon juice into it or add a drop or two of lemon essential oil. Although lemon juice is acidic, it is alkaline-forming when digested.

You can use a water flask that contains alkalizing minerals.

Water flasks that contain alkalizing minerals will alkalize your water in a few minutes. There are better options, depending on your situation and budget, but water flasks are vastly better than bottled water or even the lemon juice method. This is what we used to alkalize our drinking water during our RTW that I told you about in Chapter 5, until we wore them out and had a hard time replacing them when we were on the move overseas.

You can use a hydrogen water bottle.

Hydrogen water bottles are portable devices that alkalize water. They typically have a battery that can be recharged with a USB. One of the disadvantages of these devices is that they only produce a small volume of alkaline water at a time. As we have resumed our travels, we take these with us. They cost more than the flasks that we originally traveled with, but they're worth the investment.

The best choice is to invest in a countertop water ionizer.

When we're home, we drink water from our home water ionizer.

About nine years ago, when I started all this research and first read about changing our water, we invested in one of these household appliances, and we became zealots. We got on a mission to help as many people as possible with their health challenges, to the best of our abilities. We are still on that mission, and it all started with the discovery of countertop water ionizers.

They are that powerful.

What do water ionizers do?

There are three main effects that the water ionizers we use have on your drinking water.

The first effect, of course, is that they make the water alkaline. Dirk and I drink water that has a pH of 9.5, but a lot of people start out at 8.5 pH. The appliance allows you to adjust the pH level and work your way up the alkaline scale as your body adjusts.

Micro-clustering

The second effect of these machines is that they micro-cluster the water molecules. You know that feeling you have when you drink a lot of water, but you still feel thirsty? I've learned that this is what happens when you drink water that has large molecule clusters. The water passes through your body with less absorption than water that has small molecule clusters.

The electrolysis process of water ionizers, on the other hand, causes the water molecules to be separated into clusters of around three to six molecules per cluster instead of, say, 100. This is how ionized water penetrates your cells and tissues much more easily than "regular" water. As a result, ionized water is super effective at not only hydrating your body, but also detoxifying it.

Antioxidant

The third effect of these machines is to create water that is antioxidant. I'll confess, I never really understood why antioxidants are so good for us. You see the word "antioxidants" on so much these days, but how many people really understand why we need them?

Here's a very basic, overly simplified explanation: Free radicals in the body are electron-deficient, and they rob electrons from healthy cells. This damages the healthy cells in the process and can cause lots of health issues. Antioxidants run to the rescue and provide electrons to free radicals.

There are a lot of foods and supplements that can also provide antioxidants, but they simply can't compete with the antioxidant powerhouse that is ionized water. This antioxidant property of the water can be tested by measuring what's called its Oxidation Reduction Potential (ORP). Water with a very low negative ORP like -900 is considered to have very strong antioxidant properties. Most other water available has an ORP ranging from 0 to +400, which makes that water oxidizing.

If you drink enough ionized water, you can feel a big difference over and above how you'd feel if you drank the same amount of non-ionized water. By the way, it's also very difficult to drink as much non-ionized water as ionized water because of the micro-clustering property of ionized water.

Because your body is about 70% water, there is arguably no other single thing you can do to benefit your health that will have a bigger impact than drinking ionized water. I hope you'll try it out for yourself. I can't promise you'll be doing cartwheels, but other good things could happen. Maybe a happy dance on your way *into* the office.

Bring a full container to work and take it home empty.

When I first started drinking ionized water, I used to sneak my two-liter, rectangular container of water into the office every day and hide it in my desk drawer. It looked like a container for anti-freeze or gasoline. I was so concerned about the other lawyers looking at me funny and thinking that I had been scammed and had drunk the Kool-Aid ... um, water ... you know what I mean. Those days are long gone. I've seen this water help too many people not to shout from the rooftops all these many years later.

You're a smart lawyer, too, no doubt. You'll figure out whether this is right for you and your family. It's definitely cheaper than all that bottled water you've probably been buying. You can learn more about the water ionizers we use by visiting www.NextGenerationWater.com.

And that 3:30 p.m. slump that used to have me running to the soda machine so that I could focus a little bit longer on the fine print that covered my desk? That's long gone, too. If nothing else, I hope you'll ditch that if it sounds all too familiar to you.

Alkaline-Forming Foods

Now that you've got the skinny on alkaline water, let's get back to another way you can protect that important asset known as your health. That's by eating alkaline-forming foods.

Most food found in the average American's kitchen is unhealthy for various reasons, including the fact that it's likely to be highly acid-forming in the body. Let's face it. A lot of stuff found in the average American pantry can hardly be called food at all.

You can do better than the S.A.D. diet. Your chosen profession pretty much requires it, and you and your family deserve it.

What to Eat?

I'm sure it's no surprise that fresh fruits and vegetables are the most alkaline-forming foods. Some of the best choices include mushrooms, citrus, dates, raisins, spinach, grapefruit, tomatoes, avocado, alfalfa grass, barley grass, cucumber, kale, jicama, wheat grass, broccoli, oregano, garlic, ginger, green beans, endive, cabbage, celery, red beet, watermelon, figs, and ripe bananas. Many types of beans are also on the list, as are some nuts like almonds, chestnuts, cashews, and macadamia nuts.

Foods and food additives that contribute to acidity in the body and are best avoided or reduced include processed foods, soda, alcohol, sugar, artificial sweeteners, food coloring, and preservatives. Also highly acid-forming: animal proteins, including beef, pork, chicken, turkey, eggs, dairy products, whey, casein, and even fish and shellfish.

I was surprised to learn that some nuts, like peanuts and walnuts, are actually acid-forming, as are most types of pasta, rice, bread, and grains found in the average American household. I'm not saying you should never consume these foods. I'm just highly recommending that you at least do a trial run of consuming more alkaline-forming foods and see if you don't have more energy for such lawyerly tasks as leaping tall buildings in a single bound. This is a good place to start, but we'll talk more about other healthy choices in Chapter 7.

Happy, healthy lawyers might still be an exception to the rule, but we can change that. Give yourself a pat on the back for delving into this seldom-discussed aspect of the legal profession. Because your ability to engage fully in the practice of law, to *actually* zealously represent your client(s) day after day and to act as their trusted advisor no matter how many curve balls get thrown at you, requires you to value your own physical as well as mental well-being.

You are not easily replaceable, and your clients and your family need you. No matter what law job you decide is right for you, you sure can't be the lawyer you were born to be if you're taking your own health for granted – or, worse, resigning yourself to being that sickly "mostly-healthy" lawyer that I was.

Let's Take It to the Next Level

When you're ready to move forward, get a big glass of alkaline water, even if for now that means you're doing the lemon water method, and we'll continue the process of getting you ready to thrive in a way you may never have experienced.

dirk's corner

Bev started drinking alkaline water when we first bought our ionizer in June of 2008. She was experiencing some profound changes in her health over the course of the two years that followed. I wasn't totally on board with it, though. I drank a little, but not nearly enough to notice any difference in the way I felt.

That was during the same time that she had her corporate counsel job. I believe it was her personal health transformation that really served as the catalyst for her leaving that position. When she declared she wanted to leave the corporate gig and dive into the wellness industry instead of lawyering, that's when I really started to take the wellness stuff a little more seriously. So, I started drinking much more of the ionized water. Within just a couple of months, I noticed some significant changes as well. Enough so that I became very interested in the wellness industry, too. More about that in the next chapter, and the Bonus Chapter that you can access by visiting www.happylawyerbonuschapter.com.

If you decide to try drinking alkaline water, try to drink at least a half-ounce per pound of your body weight daily. To experience the best results, I encourage you to work up to drinking a full ounce per pound of body weight per day. In addition, try to drink it as freshly made as possible. If you can make a habit of it, we firmly believe you will feel a difference.

I also suggest you keep a food diary and write down everything you eat. Make note of which foods are acid- or alkaline-forming. Strive to have more foods on the list in the alkaline-forming column. Make a game out of it if that helps.

Bev mentioned sodas above, but I want to stress how important it is to avoid them. They are so acidic that even consuming one or two a week is enough to keep your body perpetually in an acidic state. They are about as damaging to your health as cigarettes. If you absolutely must drink sodas, seek out boutique brands with healthier ingredients. Better yet, drink kombucha. There are now kombucha-based sodas on the market, as well. Not as healthy as just kombucha, but much healthier than regular sodas. I used to drink much more soda than Bev, and quitting was very difficult for me. It was before I discovered kombucha and I weaned myself off with sweet tea.

Sports drinks are almost as unhealthy as sodas. Try organic coconut water with an added pinch of Himalayan or other healthy salt instead when exercising. This is a much healthier alternative for electrolyte replacement than neon drinks full of processed sugar or artificial sweeteners, artificial coloring, chemical flavor enhancers and preservatives, etc.

Stress is not good for us for several reasons, including causing high acidity in the body. So make time to relax, unwind, and de-stress. This is a big factor in maintaining an alkaline body.

Regarding your drinking water, at the very minimum we suggest filtering it. As Bev mentioned, bottled water will contain chemical residues from the plastic. Tap water is not a better choice. Almost all tap water contains harmful chemicals and heavy metals. In addition to other negative effects, these chemicals and metals contribute to acidity in the body. Enter your zip code into the Environmental Working Group's tap water database at www.ewg.org/tapwater to see what contaminants are in your local tap water.

chapter seven
Nourish Your Body

"To eat is a necessity, but to eat intelligently is an art."

LA ROCHEFOUCALD

t his step of the BALANCED Way™ process, Nourish Your Body, builds on Alkalize to Optimize to help you to become and project the most radiant, energetic and confident version of you as you go after your dream job and thrive in your career.

I Feel Good Enough

In Chapter 6, I told you about my shigella experience when I was in law school. Around that same time, a few family members were diagnosed with Type II diabetes and breast cancer, and my dad was struggling with Crohn's disease. Both of my maternal grandparents died within six weeks of each other around that time, too. I studied for my final Trusts exam from the hospital bedside of someone I cared about deeply while he underwent angioplasty. And one of my law school classmates went into diabetic shock and had to be rushed to the hospital *during* the bar exam. I realized at a very young age, maybe too early in life, that I was not invincible.

As a result, although I didn't really do any research on nutrition at that point in my life, as I mentioned earlier, I did jump on board with the standard American approach to healthy eating: more foods like baked chicken, whole wheat bread, low-fat milk, salad, canned tuna, deli lunch meat instead of the pre-packaged stuff, and so on. Just like most people who follow that diet, I thought I was doing it right. I raised three beautiful sons that way.

They were (and still are) young, energetic and healthy, and I felt okay most of the time. Everything was fine.

Until I discovered something better.

No More S.A.D.ness for Me

During my corporate counsel days, Dirk and I were trying to help support his dad, whose grandpa name was Cinco, in his battle with leukemia. As I said before, we aren't doctors, but by that time we'd watched my dad succumb to lung cancer just before we married. Being diagnosed with lung cancer when you've been battling Crohn's for years is no picnic. My dad had his always-doting "bride" of forty-three years, my sweet mom, who took good care of Dad and never gave up on him. He also had the love and support of our entire family.

But it wasn't enough.

Now it was Cinco and his doting bride, my big-hearted mother-in-law, who takes care of everyone. Cinco had his entire family loving and supporting him, too.

Dirk and I felt like we had to do more than just sit by and watch while Cinco appeared to be headed toward the same fate as my dad. So we did what we do: we started researching. Everything we could get our hands on. We kept open minds, which as you know is not something that we lawyers are always encouraged to do. And that's too bad.

Fortunately, we weren't afraid to think outside the box, and we left no stone unturned. I came across a book that touts itself as the "most comprehensive study on nutrition ever conducted." It's called *The China Study*, by T. Colin Campbell, PhD.

First it made me really angry, because for years I'd already been doing all of the things I thought were healthy: everything that we are all taught. And then, as I calmed down and let the information sink in, that book changed my life.

On page 244 of the book's 417 pages, Dr. Campbell suggests trying a new way of eating on a trial basis, for just one month. He says that if you don't feel better after a month, you can always go back to the way you ate before. Even though I came across the book in an effort to help Cinco, I was also sick and tired of not quite feeling myself. So I decided to accept the challenge. I love a good challenge.

Initially, Dirk made fun of me while he ate hamburgers and French fries, but I didn't care. Almost immediately, I felt so good, I knew I was on the right track for me. Until I read that book and did my own trial, I had no idea that my diet was a huge part of my problem all those years.

I mean, my diet had kept me feeling just well enough to drag myself into the office and bill my 166 hours/month when I worked for a few different law firms. My diet had provided just enough energy to get me through the morning docket, grab a quick lunch, and tackle the afternoon docket when I was at the DA's office. My diet and my obligatory morning gym ritual hadn't made me overweight or caused me to be on any medications. My blood pressure was always really low, and that made me feel tired, but that was better than having high blood pressure. My stomach always gave me problems, but *everyone* suffers from something, right? It's not like I ever called in sick. That would've been disastrous, anyway, because I don't know how I would've got caught up if I had.

As I mentioned, I successfully kept the plates spinning. My clients and bosses were always happy with me. I drove a Mercedes and lived in a nice house. My children were smiling and healthy. Sure, lawyering was mentally and sometimes physically exhausting, and I was severely depressed and sometimes losing my mind. But it never occurred to me that my diet could be part of the problem.

I think most lawyers can relate to at least some of this.

Thankfully, 30 days has turned into seven years and counting. I'll never go back to the way I ate before. For me, that S.A.D. diet had to go, and good riddance. I just didn't know it until I tried something different.

Incidentally, Dirk jumped on board about three months into my "30-day challenge," and he has never looked back either. I count my blessings every day that I am married to someone who is open-minded, supportive, and loving enough to be on this crazy health-kick journey with me. It's not always comfortable.

So, anyway, I highly recommend that, sometime during your career makeover, you make the time to read *The China Study* and go to www.happylawyerbook.com to access our A-Z Wellness Guide. I know it'll benefit you during your career transition and beyond.

I told you in Chapter 6 that we would dig deeper into ways to maintain the physical and mental health that are foundational if you are to become the happy lawyer you are meant to be. What you put in your body is essential.

Plant-Based vs. Omnivore

I recommend you keep animal proteins to no more than 10% of your overall caloric intake. Better yet, eliminate them altogether.

Why?

The cold hard truth is, people with diets consisting of more than 10% animal proteins are much more susceptible to numerous degenerative diseases. The average American has a diet that consists of a whopping 40% or more of animal proteins, with the remainder being mostly processed foods and only a small amount of fresh, whole foods. It's no mystery why disease rates have soared in recent decades among Americans.

That Protein Thing

Now, I'm not here to tell you that going vegan is the end-all, be-all when it comes to diet. I mean, Skittles and Oreos are vegan, but no one's touting them as health foods. I like to emphasize a "whole plant-based" diet versus a "vegan" diet for better energy and overall wellness and vitality.

The most common misconception about a plant-based diet is that you need to consume animal proteins to get enough protein. I happen to believe, and it's been well researched, that this is a myth and that you can get all the protein you need from plants.

If you're old enough, you may have been exposed to this radical concept as a kid. Popeye knew that eating spinach made him strong. Now I know Popeye doesn't come to mind when you envision the lawyer you are meant to be, but I'll bet he'd have the stamina to get through stacks of contracts and back-to-back conference calls even after a bout with Bluto. Just a thought.

As it turns out, kale, dandelion greens, collard greens, and other leafy greens are good sources of protein, too, as well as nuts, beans and legumes. And I was surprised to learn that a large avocado has more usable protein than an eight-ounce steak.

If you know that you can't stop eating meat even for 30 days, try what some call the "reducetarian" approach, the 10% guideline I mentioned above. See how you feel.

Organic or Not?

Yes, organic.

All food used to be organic. Before the introduction of chemicals and genetic modification into the food supply, organic food was simply known as "food."

What exactly qualifies a food as organic? In a nutshell, it is food that has not been genetically modified or had any chemical fertilizers or pesticides applied to it. Foods that are labeled "USDA Organic," in theory, meet these criteria.

The system is not perfect, though. There are foods out there with that logo on the label that aren't 100% organic. In general, these are healthier than their non-organic counterparts; however, something like a non-organic avocado is going to be healthier than organic potato chips.

When it comes to non-organic fruits and vegetables, some are better than others regarding pesticide levels. In general, if you are peeling the skin like with a banana or avocado, it is going to have fewer pesticides compared to something like grapes or apples where you usually eat the skin. However, even if you are peeling the skin, it will have pesticides that will have penetrated it and pesticides that arrived via the roots from the contaminated soil.

Chemicals in your food end up in your body. Some pass through, but others lodge in your cells and tissues. They can accumulate in your body and over time may end up causing some serious health issues.

I have never met a lawyer who has time for that.

Juice or Smoothie?

Yes. Both. First, let's talk about juicing.

Vegetable juicing is absolutely one of the best ways to get nutrients into your body, and it can help you to look and feel awesome in a relatively short period of time. One time, Dirk and I hosted a viewing of the film *Fat, Sick and Nearly Dead* in our wellness center. One of our attendees, our good friend Mark, got inspired and went on a month-long juice fast. He lost about 50 pounds, had tons of energy, and had incredibly glowing skin. He became an inspiration for so many others and looked years younger in such a short period of time. Granted, a month of nothing but green juice and ionized water probably didn't feel like a short period of time for Mark, but he remained committed to rebooting and gaining control of his health.

Although he's not a lawyer, Mark worked for the same corporation where I had served as corporate counsel, and his job presented similar challenges. Every day that he was on that juice fast, he toted his small Playmate cooler full of green juice to work, and he stuck with the juice fast despite all the temptations and reasons to quit. (Have you *had* the Mexican food in San Antonio?!) Always a stand-out employee anyway, Mark related that he felt sharper, more productive, and – after the first couple of days – much more energetic than when he was still consuming his pre-juicing S.A.D. diet.

One downside to juicing is that it can be time-consuming. The good news is that juice bars are becoming much more popular now, and new ones are opening frequently. If you are simply too busy to do your own juicing, try to find the nearest juice bar where you live or work. If they use organic produce, that's a bonus, but drinking non-organic juice is still better than not drinking any green juice at all.

Why "Green" Juice?

My general rule of thumb when it comes to juicing is that I prefer to juice vegetables (separating the fiber from the juice), but to blend fruit or eat it whole. In other words, I don't juice fruits. There are a couple of reasons for this.

First, most fruit is very high in sugar content. You want the fiber with it to slow down the sugar absorption. If you get a sugar high, you're going to crash. Again, I know you don't have time for that.

Also, the fiber in fruit is digestible, whereas the fiber in vegetables is not. If you eat one salad a day, it can give you your necessary fiber, depending upon what else you eat. Otherwise, vegetable fibers can actually impede the body's ability to get some nutrients from the plant.

It's fine to juice an apple with your vegetables; but, generally speaking, you'll want your juice to be as green as possible.

What Vegetables to Juice, Then?

Remember that, ideally, you'll want to juice only organic vegetables.

Some of my favorite things to juice are dandelion greens, wheat grass, and kale. Romaine lettuce, spinach, collard greens, mustard greens, chard, and ginger are also highly nutritious. Beets are excellent for cleansing the blood. Make sure you also juice the greens from the beets, rather than throwing them away, because they're highly nutritious, too. And cilantro and parsley are good for detoxing mercury and other heavy metals.

Feel free to switch it up and add things like celery, broccoli, bell peppers, asparagus, cucumbers, squash, etc. to provide your body with a variety of nutrients on an ongoing basis. As you get used to the taste, you'll tolerate the bitterness of vegetable juice much better than when your first start out. In the beginning, you may need to add more carrot, beet, or apple juice to your greens and other bitter vegetables, and gradually reverse that ratio in favor of more versus fewer leafy greens.

Juicing for the Win

The foods I just recommended you juice are not my favorites because they taste good when you juice them. They're my favorites because they leave me feeling so unstoppable. I decided a long time ago that I would not always allow my taste buds to dictate what happens with the rest of my body, so I make decisions that I know a lot of people don't want to make.

Want to know a little secret? I believe this actually gives me an edge. Even though most of my practice these days revolves around uncontested, transactional matters (Thank God!), I do still have some hotly contested and document-intensive matters come across my desk. I think I'm a pretty smart lawyer, but that's not what gives me the biggest advantage most of the time. Most of the time, it's my two secret weapons: 1) I smile a lot and remain totally relaxed and calm; and 2) I can stay sharp and focused on even the most tedious of matters – basically pass the endurance test – every time. I hope you'll give it glow and try vegetable juicing. If you're still feeling unsure about how to do it, our A-Z Wellness Guide can help. You can get it at www.happylawyerbook.com.

Smoothies

There are lots of ways to make a healthy smoothie that tastes good; but apparently, most of the big-chain smoothie shops haven't figured this out. You can do better, and the good news about smoothies is that they're super quick and easy to make at home.

As with juicing, there are lots of recipes and resources online, but you probably don't need them. Toss some fresh or frozen organic berries into your high-speed blender, add unsweetened, non-dairy milk (I like organic coconut milk), part of a banana or avocado if you want, and maybe a scoop of vegan (not whey), non-GMO meal replacement powder. You can also add ice (which I don't do because I usually start with frozen fruits, which are cold enough for me), as well as other "add-ons," like a bit of hemp seed, spirulina, or other superfoods.

You can do this in less time than you'd spend in the Starbucks or McDonald's drive-through on your way to the office. And slurping down those sugary lattes or munching on that sausage biscuit isn't really what someone who values their health as one of their greatest assets would do anyway. That's just going to leave you feeling sluggish in the afternoon, and likely feeling way worse than that after years of making it a habit.

Raw vs. Cooked Foods

I recommend you increase your intake of raw fruits and vegetables until your diet consists of about 50-80% raw food – whatever feels best for you. Here are a few reasons why:

- Raw food is in its natural state, allowing your body to derive more nutritional benefit from it vs. cooked food. Live enzymes and vitamins offer the best nutrition.

- Eating an organic, mostly raw food diet allows your body to eliminate more toxins than when you eat mostly cooked food.

- You will likely have more energy, notice improvement in your skin, feel younger, and reduce food cravings by consuming more raw vs. cooked foods.

You might be surprised by how interesting and delicious raw food can be. Some of my most popular recipes throughout the years have been my raw food creations. In fact, being a raw foodie has become such a passion of mine that I studied to become a raw food chef, just for fun. People are often surprised to learn that healthy food can taste that good. Mmmmm….

Of course, you don't need a recipe to grab a piece of fruit or a vegetable and eat it. When Dirk and I were finally able to visit the Fijian island of Taveuni after so many years of me day-dreaming about it, we stayed in a beautiful little house right on the beach. The caretakers for the property, Joe and his wife Vini, lived in the house just in front of the one where we stayed. Every morning, Joe would fill up a huge bowl of fruit from the island, mostly passion fruit, bananas and papayas, and leave it on our kitchen counter. On our last day on the island, he finally climbed the tree in our front yard and brought down a coconut for each of us. He cut the coconuts open and plunked a straw into each one. He also carved a small spoon for each of us from the coconut shell. Now that's living. I loved being mostly a fruitetarian during our too-short of a stay on that island, but I wasn't always so keen on raw fruits. Your palate can learn to love raw fruits and vegetables, and your body will thank you.

Whole Foods vs. Processed Foods

Let's face it: the majority of food in most U.S. grocery stores shouldn't really even be called food. It is more accurate to call this stuff "food-like products." These food-like-products are created by processing original foods to the point of not only losing their nutrients, but also transforming into "food" that is very unhealthy. You are always going to be better off eating food that is as close to what it was when it came out of the ground, just like we did in Fiji. So are your children.

A general rule of thumb at the grocery store is that whole foods that are the least processed are around the perimeter of the store, and the most highly processed foods are in the center. There are exceptions, of course. Another good rule of thumb is that the healthiest food doesn't have a label and doesn't come in a package. This is one of the many reasons why we love to shop at farmer's markets.

Fermented Foods

Your body is a metropolis of micro-organisms. Keeping them in proper balance is essential to good health. Fermented foods are foods that have gone through a lacto-fermentation process in which lactic acid is created as a result of natural bacteria feeding on the sugar and starch in the food. This process serves to preserve the food, as well as create B vitamins, beneficial enzymes, Omega-3 fatty acids, and assorted strains of probiotics.

Fermented foods also help optimize your immune system. It is estimated that 80% of your immune system is actually located in your gut. Probiotics play a critical role in the development and functioning of the part of your immune system that is in your digestive tract.

As I mentioned before, and I know you know this: You don't have time to be sick.

If you're not used to eating fermented foods or drinking kombucha already, begin with about a half-cup of a fermented food or beverage per day and work your way up. Some fermented foods I eat regularly include kimchi, miso, and tempeh. If you've never heard of this stuff, don't fret. Our A-Z Wellness Guide can help you.

A word of warning, though: You will probably be called out if you start keeping kimchi, which tends to be pretty stinky, in the office refrigerator and eating it at work. You might do best to eat it at home and/or outdoors on a nice day.

Essential Oils

Okay, I'm an admitted EO fanatic, so I'd be remiss if I didn't share this information with you, too.

Essential oils are basically the lifeblood of plants. When it comes to nutrition and healing, the power of plants has been known for eons; and essential oils are the most potent part of the plant. They have been used for thousands of years for lots of purposes. Did you know that there are 54 essential oils mentioned in the Bible?

A lot of people think of essential oils just for aromatherapy, but they can support your healthy lifestyle and help nourish your body in so many ways, as skin care, perfume, pain relief, hormone balancers, nutritional supplements, and so much more.

Honestly, I just can't imagine being without EOs in my life, which is why we even made room for dozens of them in our backpacks and used them frequently during our RTW.

Other than that, though, I already told you that one of my secret weapons as a lawyer is that I'm always smiling and always calm. Perhaps not unlike you, I definitely have my moments when I'd like to reach across the conference room table and smack someone. I largely attribute my ability to contain myself and remain happy, calm, and peaceful to my obsession with EOs. Of course, meditation, exercise, and morning pages help, too. But I never underestimate the power of my EOs for helping me stay calm, for keeping stress away, and for providing the confidence I need when I've got an important meeting or seminar coming up.

I even diffuse EOs in my office. Clients love them, too.

If you decide to use EOs to help diminish any desire you may have to lunge at a snarky co-worker or opposing counsel, or for any other reason, just remember that not all oils on the market are the same. Unfortunately, most are adulterated with cheaper oils and synthetic ingredients. I've also learned that the majority of essential oils on the market are extracted with hexane. This is the cheapest method for oil extraction, and it contaminates the oil with hexane residue.

The highest quality oils on the market are steam-distilled. The adage "you get what you pay for" is especially true with essential oils.

For more information on therapeutic-grade essential oils and for the use of EOs on a variety of topics ranging from weight management to hormone balance to green living, to staying calm and maintaining focus and clarity, check out www.OilyTravelers.com.

Nutritional Supplements

First of all, who should take nutritional supplements? The answer is, almost everyone. This includes probably every lawyer I've ever met.

If you consider the depletion of nutrients in our food supply, it is easy to see how challenging it can be to get all of the nutrients your body needs for optimum health without supplementation.

To me, taking the right nutritional supplements is a no-brainer for helping me stay healthy and serve my clients at the highest level that I'm capable of. I definitely notice the difference when I forget and go too long without taking them.

I recommend you look for organic, whole-plant supplements. These contain the whole spectrum of nutrients in a food, instead of fractionated versions of a vitamin. Fractionated vitamins are isolated components that are processed differently by the body than the full version of the nutrient.

When you juice vegetables like we talked about earlier, the nutrients from pounds of plants can be concentrated into a single glass of juice by eliminating the plant fiber. Whole-plant supplements are made by taking this process a step further and eliminating the water. If that glass of juice is dehydrated, the leftover powder is highly concentrated nutrients that can be put into capsules. In a nutshell, this is how whole-plant supplements are made.

Another general rule of thumb with supplements is that capsules are going to be much better than tablets. A tablet needs a binding agent to hold it together, which is the bulk of the tablet. Some tablets will pass completely through your digestive system before becoming fully dissolved. Some cheap ones may not even fully dissolve before exiting you. Once capsules dissolve, the nutrients are absorbed much more quickly and efficiently.

Deciding which supplements are right for you depends upon your overall health and your daily diet. If you drink vegetable juice regularly, your nutritional needs are going to be different than those of a meat and potatoes type of eater. Things like nutritional blood analysis and bloodwork can help you determine what some of those needs are.

At a minimum, I generally recommend a good daily multivitamin, a probiotic, krill oil, vitamin D3, and – for vegans – vitamin B-12 (methylcobalamin is preferable to cyanocobalamin). Dirk and I also take a high-quality turmeric and bluegreen algae supplement every day for additional support.

I also recommend taking plant enzymes to help you digest cooked food. A good way to test enzymes for their effectiveness is to perform the oatmeal or pudding test. Open a capsule of your enzyme and add the contents of it to a cup of pudding or prepared oatmeal. If the enzymes are effective, then the oatmeal or pudding should totally liquefy after stirring for about 30 seconds to a minute or so.

DNA-Customized and Anti-Aging Supplements

Lots of us in this profession are into customization, right? Custom-made suits, furniture, homes, and more. If you want a supplement that's really customized for you, they are available based on the results of DNA testing. I think this is a cool idea.

When I did this, I found out that I have a genetic predisposition for issues related to cardiovascular health, yet another reason why I watch my diet very closely and maintain a mostly vegetarian diet. My mother-in-law, incidentally, had the best genetic profile of anyone the company we went with had ever tested. As my oldest son once said about her, "She's one of the youngest people I know." Well put. At the age of 79, she's not slowing down anytime soon.

So, yes, some people are blessed with "good genes," and may have less of a predisposition for certain things than the rest of us. Unfortunately, many people seem to believe they are victims of their genes and that ending up with a certain disease is completely out of their control. On the contrary, while we certainly can have genetic predispositions that make us more or less susceptible to certain diseases or conditions, it's been proven that we can often affect the expression of our genes with proper nutrition.

Talk about a super-duper secret weapon and placing a high value on your health as one of your greatest assets as a lawyer. Customization might be for you.

There's one more type of supplement I want to tell you about if you have the attitude, "I ain't getting any younger." In addition to DNA-customized supplements, a new generation of anti-aging supplements is available in the marketplace. These supplements are designed to slow or prevent telomere degeneration. Telomere caps are basically the enzymes that form the protective layer at each end of your DNA strands that keep the strands tight. As we age, these deteriorate and the strands start to unravel, which makes your DNA less efficient at cell replication. Even though every cell in our bodies is completely new and regenerated every few years, our cells aren't perfect copies of previous cells due to this process.

This is why our appearance changes as we age. It's like making an analog recording of something, then making another analog recording of that recording, and so on. Each time the sound and/or video quality deteriorates. It's the same with your cells. Telomere enzyme supplements are designed to keep your telomere caps in top shape to prevent the unraveling of your DNA strands. This keeps your body reproducing current versions of your cells rather than the slightly deteriorated versions that they normally would.

I said at the beginning, the BALANCED Way™ is a mind, body, and spirit approach to law and life, and I know we've gone deep. I want to take a moment to honor your commitment to your health and hopefully for your recognition that none of us in this profession can become the lawyer we are meant to be without it. My message is not one that lawyers or anyone else necessarily wants to hear, but I believe our proper role as trusted advisors in society is far too important to continue to ignore the elephant in the room. That is simply inexcusable when we know we can do better – for ourselves, for our families, and for our clients.

I hope you'll incorporate some of or all of the recommendations in this chapter into your life as you go through your career makeover and beyond. Keep journaling and jotting down how you feel, noting in your food log what you're eating and drinking. Write down any differences that you're noticing in your energy, focus, and mood, as well as challenges and any new discoveries about how this is affecting your job search and/or your current position.

Take a moment to check in with yourself, drink plenty of healthy water, walk around a little bit, keep asking and allowing, and ... most of all ... breathe.

dirk's corner

Bev mentioned that reading *The China Study* changed her life. I didn't know it at the time, but it was going to change my life, too. As she said, for the first few months after she had switched to a plant-based diet, I was mostly laughing at her while eating the same way I always had. In the past, I often joked that simply looking at a cow made my mouth water, and that I could never give up eating meat.

However, as she mentioned, we were trying to help my dad in his struggle with leukemia. I was starting to learn a lot, and began to realize that the way I ate was not leading me down a desirable path. On a long road-trip to California, I did most of the driving while she read *The China Study* to me.

By the time we returned to San Antonio, I had decided to take the 30-day challenge as well. And I kept going. Without even trying, I "accidentally" lost about 45 pounds. I had so much more energy. Even my volleyball teammates noticed a difference in my game. I don't always follow a "perfect" diet, but it is radically better than it was before that time. I have kept the weight off, and have far fewer aches and pains on a day-to-day basis than I did before. Between the dietary changes and the ionized water consumption, I feel like I became a different person. Thanks, Bev!

It's the foods we eat daily or several times a week that are going to have the biggest impact on our health, or lack thereof. Using that food diary we've mentioned before, identify your weaknesses, as well as the foods you consume most frequently, and seek out healthier alternatives that leave you satisfied.

Two of the easiest things to change that most people use very frequently are your choice of salt and sweetener. For salt, switch to pink Himalayan or Real Salt®, or grey Celtic sea salt. In other words, salt that is the least processed and which still contains the full spectrum of minerals in it, instead of being stripped down to about 98% sodium chloride plus some chemical residue from the processing like regular table salt. For sweetener, use 100% organic stevia (most stevia products contain other ingredients, too, and are not organic), or raw organic local honey when stevia isn't a good match. Stevia is actually very healthy. Raw, organic honey is healthy to a degree, but use it sparingly due to its sugar content.

Do you like to eat pasta often? Switch to brown rice or einkorn pasta instead. Or, better yet, spiralized zucchini.

Cut the crap food out of your life, like processed foods, artificial sweeteners, and chemical-laden foodstuffs. When you start eating cleaner, you will probably find that foods such as these will give you a headache or food hangover.

Try to plan and begin preparation of your meals before you are hungry. Otherwise, you are more likely to make unhealthy choices just to not feel hungry.

Be a label hawk. Become familiar with the unhealthiest ingredients and avoid food with those ingredients. Go organic, and use the Fooducate app (www.fooducate.com) when grocery shopping. Look for foods with short ingredient lists. The longer the ingredient list, the higher likelihood that the food is full of chemicals. If you don't know what an ingredient is, assume it's unhealthy until you research it and determine otherwise.

Lastly, don't try to do it all at once or you are very likely to fail. Change an item or two at a time, and stretch out the changes over several months. Baby steps will get you to the destination more surely than attempting to arrive via leaps and bounds.

For more info and tips, be sure to check out our A-Z Wellness Guide, available at www.happylawyerbook.com.

chapter eight
Cleanse for Clarity

"If we are creating ourselves all the time, then it is never too late to begin creating the bodies we want instead of the ones we mistakenly assume we are stuck with."

DEEPAK CHOPRA

b y the time you get to this step of the BALANCED Way™ process, your body will be telling you what it needs. Don't forget to listen to it. (Unless it's telling you all too often that you need a burger and fries, in which case, I recommend you repeat Steps 2-5.) Make sure you're putting good thoughts, healthy water, and the right nutrients into it. Don't give up.

You might also start to notice at this point that your mind feels sharper, and maybe you've begun making decisions with greater confidence, as all of these steps that we've covered so far have been working in tandem. To keep your mind sharp and to maintain clarity so that you can continue on your path to becoming the lawyer you were born to be, I want to take this health-kick stuff up one more level with you.

You see, when it comes to maintaining your most vibrant physical body, there are basically three components you'll want to focus on:

- Taking in the proper nutrition, which we've already covered;

- Exercising, which we'll talk about in Chapter 9; and,

- Eliminating toxins from your body and reducing the accumulation of more toxins. That's what this step is about.

Keep in mind that some parts of this step can get a little intense, so take it easy. You don't have to do it all at once. Nor should you.

Cleansing: It's Not Just for January Anymore

Before doing a heavy-metal detox, which we'll talk about in parts of this chapter, you should study the methods thoroughly and proceed slowly. Pulling too much out of your tissues too fast can be difficult for your body to deal with all at once and make you feel really lousy until the toxins are fully expelled. I recommend you consult with a qualified medical professional before engaging in any heavy-metal detox protocol.

When detoxing, always make sure you are well-hydrated.

Once you do a thorough cleanse and develop a routine that reduces the toxins you're putting back into your body, you may decide you want to stick with your new regimen well past your career transformation – perhaps for life. That's not unusual. I hope you do.

It feels awesome to have so much clarity and energy, to know that you're in control of your own environment and well-being, and to look and feel like a million bucks.

Secret weapons!

Flushing Out the Toxins

In the first part of this step, I'll teach you ways to get rid of the sludge that's just sitting there, not serving any beneficial purpose, and likely causing all kinds of inflammation and other problems. The beauty of this is that some of these ways to detox could also fall under the category of "self-care," which is always a good idea anyway.

I hope you know by now that you can't just run on that hamster wheel day after day without taking some time for yourself. Some of these first few ideas are as beneficial from purely a relaxation and "time for me" standpoint as they are from a flush-out-the-toxins standpoint. Good thing, because I'm guessing efficiency is important to you, and here's an opportunity to kill two birds with one stone.

Ways to Eliminate Stored Toxins

Massage

One of the easiest – and possibly the most enjoyable – ways to eliminate some of those toxins is by getting a massage. In addition to many other health benefits, massages are a great way to stimulate the lymphatic system and help tissues absorb oxygen and nutrients. This aids not only in detoxification, but also in many overall body processes.

Infrared Sauna

Heat treatments have been employed for healing the body for thousands of years. Infrared saunas can leave you feeling so happy and sure of yourself, as if you've cleared the cobwebs from your brain. Everyone's experience is different, but I recommend you try it out.

The way infrared saunas work is they emit infrared light waves that create heat in the body, causing you to sweat and release toxins. They differ from regular saunas in that the light penetrates into your body tissues and generates heat much deeper than radiant heat from warmed air surrounding you. These saunas can generate infrared wavelengths in the near, middle, and far range. Near-infrared wavelengths are best known for increasing immune function and healing wounds. Middle-infrared is best known for muscle relaxation and improved circulation. Far-infrared is best known for detoxification purposes.

Epsom Salt Baths

Not only are Epsom salt baths relaxing, but they are also another great way to detox. They are one of the best ways to end a long, stressful day. They provide your body with magnesium sulfate, which draws out toxins, eases stress, and helps improve sleep and concentration. Add a few drops of therapeutic-grade essential oil such as lavender and soak for 20 minutes. Ahhh….

Skin Brushing

Your skin is your largest organ. It's also known as your third kidney, and it's a vital component of the detoxification process. Skin brushing can help to improve lymphatic drainage and reduce cellulite. Using a dry skin brush on dry skin, brush in a circular motion, starting with the extremities and moving towards the heart to improve blood flow towards the heart. Then rinse off all those dead skin cells. OMG. It feels so rejuvenating!

Earthing

Eliminating free radicals from the body is an important part of the detoxification process, too. As we talked about in Chapter 6, antioxidants are one way to eliminate free radicals because they help the body by providing extra electrons. There are other ways to do this, too.

One easy way is the practice of what's called "earthing." It's accomplished by walking barefoot on the ground, or indoors on natural surfaces such as hardwood, concrete, or tile floors. The earth's surface contains a limitless and continuously renewed supply of free electrons. By connecting with it, our body absorbs some of these electrons that aid in the elimination of free radicals from the body.

A popular way to "earth" is to walk on the beach barefoot. Most people find a nice stroll on the beach to be a wonderfully relaxing experience for various reasons anyway. This could be one of the reasons, and they just don't know it. If you don't live at the beach, you can still do this in your own yard or at a nearby park.

Just think how different the legal profession would be if more lawyers took time to "earth" on a regular basis. Try it on weekends, after work, during lunch, or whenever you can squeeze in as few as ten or fifteen minutes. In my own experience, this practice has a tendency to provide perspective and an opportunity to regain control of my thoughts. In fact, when timed right, it can keep me from firing off an email that should not be sent anyway.

Oil Pulling

Another easy method for helping to eliminate toxins from your body is through the ancient Ayurvedic practice of oil pulling. This is done by swishing a tablespoon or so of oil in your mouth for 10 to 20 minutes and then spitting it out. You do not swallow the oil.

Although it's recently grown in popularity, oil pulling has been used for centuries. Proponents say that by helping to eliminate toxins, oil pulling not only helps improve oral health, but it can also help prevent heart disease, reduce inflammation, and boost the immune system.

I'm not sure about all of that, although far be it from me to rule any of it out. When I asked my trusted, holistic dentist about oil pulling, he didn't agree or disagree with any of the above; but he did share his belief that oil pulling on a regular basis does seem to help whiten teeth and that possibly people who do it on a regular basis have fewer cavities. Those comments, combined with how clean my mouth feels after I oil pull, are reasons enough for me to do it on a somewhat regular basis. If you're going to miss work and have to make up the hours and/or catch up on what you missed, I believe it should be because you're out of the office having fun. It should not be because you're sick or have a cavity.

And besides, we all exude more confidence when we feel good about our smile, so I always recommend it. Why not?

Here's how I do it:

I take a small spoonful of coconut oil and then I add a drop or two of a therapeutic-grade, anti-microbial essential oil for added benefits, and a drop or two of orange essential oil for whitening. After 20 minutes of swishing, I spit out the oil, rinse and gargle with about an ounce or two of Himalayan salt water, spit that out, and then brush my teeth with a non-toxic toothpaste.

If you try it, although it sounds gross, you really should spit the oil out in the trashcan instead of the sink so it doesn't clog the pipes.

To summarize, potential benefits: nicer smile; more confidence when you smile (which is part of your secret weapon); chance of eliminating toxins from your body, which if ignored might lead to more serious health issues; and chance of preventing cavities so you don't have to miss work because of a toothache or worse (and can save those out-of-office days for fun).

Potential negatives: you may have to empty out your trashcan more often.

Just try it.

Colon Cleanse

So now we're increasing in difficulty and for some people, maybe moving up the weirdness scale, too. In fact, this recommendation seems to freak so many people out that I'm a little reluctant to tell you about it. But, whatever. I get colonoscopies done every 10 years to keep my mom happy, and the gastroenterologist pretty much laughs me out of there as if I'm wasting his time, and then tells me to come back in another 10 years. So, I feel like we might as well take it up a notch and talk about the dreaded colon cleanse, because I do feel like that's a factor working in my favor, as well as in the favor of many others.

Please don't think I'm picking on you because you're a lawyer. After all, I am, too. The truth is that many people, if not most people, have at least some impacted fecal matter that inhibits optimum colon performance, meaning that they are literally (partially) full of you-know-what. Ew. Sorry/not sorry to bring it up. As I keep saying, I know you're a smart lawyer and will decide to work that, y'know … stuff … out.

The purpose of a colon cleanse is to help the digestive system function at its maximum level of efficiency and to clean out any impacted fecal matter that may be stubbornly holding position. Your body has a natural process to make this happen, of course, but colon cleanses can greatly enhance that process.

There are two main categories of colon cleanses: those that must be done in a clinic and administered by a professional, and those that can be done at home.

The clinical version is typically called a colonic or colon hydrotherapy. Depending on where you live, you might need a prescription to have this done. I'm not averse to this method; I just know that it costs more and is more time-consuming than doing a DIY cleanse at home. Granted, it probably yields more effective results, but I haven't personally felt the need to go there just yet. You can decide for yourself whether to give it a try.

The home version of a colon cleanse is typically an enema. This can be done with just plain water or with Himalayan salt water. Be sure to at least use purified, filtered water. The use of ionized water is better.

Then there's the coffee enema, which is part of the Gerson Therapy as detailed in the documentary *The Beautiful Truth*. It was accidentally discovered during World War II in a German army hospital that was cut off from supplies and later incorporated into the Gerson Institute's holistic cancer protocol. Coffee enemas have been used for decades as an inexpensive way to cleanse the colon. And they can also yield other positive benefits, including, as reported by almost everyone I know who has done this regularly, glowing skin. Bonus!

Obviously, you'll want to use organic coffee. The way it works in general terms is that the caffeine in the coffee travels directly to the liver and stimulates the liver to produce more bile, which aids in the faster expulsion of toxins. When coffee has been drunk, your digestive system processes the caffeine and it doesn't have the same effect.

I know it's gross to talk about, and maybe you can't fathom what this has to do with your career makeover – until you do it. People report often that they feel energized and have a much better sense of clarity when they do it.

Diatomaceous Earth

DE is a very fine powder comprised of the fossils of really small aquatic organisms known as diatoms. It's considered to be a powerful, natural detoxifying agent that can kill viruses and parasites and can help cleanse the blood by absorbing harmful toxins. DE is also known for cleansing the digestive tract and boosting liver function, as well as acting as a heavy metal detox agent. And, finally, some say that DE helps improve ligaments, joints, and bone health, as well as protecting skin, nails, and teeth.

If you want to give it a try, mix a teaspoon in a glass of ionized water daily, and then chase it with another glass of pure, ionized water. Work your way up to a tablespoon of DE per day. Continue for at least two weeks for an effective parasite cleanse – especially if you have pets, or eat raw or undercooked flesh like sushi and rare steak.

Bentonite Clay

BC has a very similar effect as DE, but is composed of volcanic ash. It has been used for hundreds of years in cleansing regimens. It also is loaded with lots of beneficial minerals. Among other benefits, BC is known to help expel toxins like mercury, cadmium, lead, and benzene, making it another important part of a heavy-metal detox.

My colleague Teri makes a facial mask with BC and applies it about once a week. She's 45, and she has a gorgeous, youthful skin tone. BC helps to maintain a more youthful appearance because it helps to tighten the skin, shrink pores, and regenerate skin tissue resulting in fewer wrinkles.

Cilantro and Other Herbs

There are many herbs that help the body detox. As we talked about when we covered juicing in Chapter 7, cilantro is one of the best known of these. Others include milk thistle, dandelion, red clover, stinging nettle, burdock root, ground ivy, and neem. Heavy metals such as lead, mercury, cadmium, and arsenic can accumulate in the body over time, and it's a good idea to cleanse the body of them regularly. If you consume seafood, there's a good chance you have mercury accumulating in your cells.

If you don't know what looking and feeling younger and cleansing have to do with your career transition, you might already have all the confidence and vitality you need to land your dream job and thrive in it every day. For the rest of you, don't be afraid to incorporate some of these recommendations as part of your career makeover.

A family friend who's in the midst of his own makeover recently posted on Facebook about his discovery of DE, apple cider vinegar, and other holistic remedies. He's losing weight, feeling healthy, and is glad to know he's setting a good example for his daughter. Mostly, he's developed a commitment to living a long, healthy life so he can enjoy his daughter and future generations.

Lots of lawyers can learn from his example.

Now that you've eliminated a lot of junk, here are some ways to minimize putting it all back in. You've learned some ways to Cleanse for Clarity and overall wellness; I want to help you maintain that healthy state. When you eliminate toxins from your body, it only does so much good if you keep re-toxifying yourself.

Ditch & Switch Your Toxic Health and Beauty Products

It starts with what you're putting on your skin, and I have to tell you, I love my makeup. I can rough it with the best of them, but I also love my girly-girl side. Sometimes I enjoy my supposedly sophisticated lawyer side, too, which used to buy expensive makeup because only the best would do. So when I read a book called *Not Just a Pretty Face: The Ugly Side of the Beauty Industry*, I got almost as angry as when I read *The China Study*. Once again, I'd been duped. *Not Just a Pretty Face* exposes the $35 billion, highly toxic, and unregulated cosmetics industry in this country and reveals some of the beauty industry's toxic secrets. It's scandalous. Maybe like you, I'd been loyal to my favorite cosmetic brands for years, and they'd let me down big time.

After I read that book and realized that I'd been slathering carcinogens on my face for decades, using products containing ingredients that the beauty industry knows are linked to the big C word and other health complications, I threw all of my cosmetics out and started over with lesser-known, non-toxic health and beauty products. Much of what I use is totally DIY.

I'm not going to tell you that I instantly felt better or healthier after making the switch, but I can honestly say that after a couple of weeks if not sooner, skin problems I'd had since I was a teenager were gone. It's an indication there's something good going on inside when the outside is glowing. As I mentioned, our skin is our largest organ. And I experienced other improvements over time that, using my own common sense and deductive reasoning skills, I could only link back to these changes I'd made in my beauty regimen.

Before I got educated about this, I was like a lot of people who treat their skin like it's some sort of impenetrable barrier. I paid no attention whatsoever to the ingredients found in the products I used, and I am embarrassed to tell you that I got a Saks Fifth Avenue credit card just for my cosmetic purchases. Not the wisest choice I've ever made.

The truth of the matter is that your skin is very permeable, and what you put on it is likely to end up inside your body, no matter how much you spend on that moisturizer or foundation. To make matters worse, these substances are bypassing your digestive system altogether and entering directly into your bloodstream. When you eat toxins, at least some of them will be buffered and expelled by your digestive system. Are the products that are coming into contact with your skin moving you towards better or poorer health? Do you know the answer?

Valuing your health, as any lawyer interested in reaching her highest potential would, includes educating yourself about the effects of what you're putting on your body, as well as in your body. Do your homework.

If your makeup comes from one of the well-known brands, there likely are ingredients in your products that can wreak havoc on your health and cause all kinds of problems. And the cosmetics companies *know* this. Apparently, some of them just don't care and will actually exploit your desire to do good by splashing pink ribbons on their products. If you are as loyal to your brand as I was to mine, this concept might cause some cognitive dissonance. But as I've said and will say again, you're a smart lawyer. I have no doubt that you'll do your own research. And then if you decide to make a change, get our A-Z Wellness Guide at www.happylawyerbook.com, if you want more information on how to replace things that are in your cosmetic bag with healthier versions of the same things. I promise, you will still look gorgeous and feel at least as confident.

Your New Signature Fragrance

"Okay, I can talk myself into switching out my makeup, but what about my favorite fragrance?"

Unfortunately, chemical-laden perfumes aren't a healthy choice, either. Not only are they not good for you, but they can also cause problems for people within your vicinity who may be sensitive to the chemicals contained in most perfumes. This is becoming known as the "new second-hand smoke."

Essential oils are a much better choice. Not only do many of them smell wonderful and work really well as a perfume, they will also have positive effects that no perfume can match, as I talked about in Chapter 7. This should be a relatively easy change to make. Remember to use only therapeutic-grade essential oils, so you don't end up replacing one type of toxic, adulterated fragrance with another.

While We're on the Subject of Smelling Good….

You know the adage, "Never let them see you sweat"? I wholeheartedly agree that that is sage advice for any lawyer, but why stop there? It's not healthy to *never* sweat, but my recommendation is to never let them *smell* you sweat.

Deodorants work by killing odor-causing bacteria. There are many natural deodorants that work really well, or you can DIY. Anti-microbial essential oils work well for this, too. Unfortunately, there isn't a natural antiperspirant. The antiperspirant part of what are usually dual deodorant and antiperspirant products uses aluminum to plug your pores and prevent sweating. This is a double whammy. When you plug up those pores, not only are you preventing toxins from leaving your body, you are also adding aluminum to the mix.

I use a natural deodorant daily. How can I get away with this and still always smell good? (I promise, I do.) Believe it or not, it's a combination of everything I've shared with you up to this point: lots of water, proper diet, essential oils, and elimination of toxins. It's like another well-kept "secret." You really don't have to choose between toxic, carcinogenic antiperspirants and smelling like a hippie. Who knew?

Household Products

Another thing I'm a zealot about is replacing the usual, toxic household products with healthier options that are just as effective and also smell wonderful. Since these bathroom, kitchen, and laundry products don't affect your taste buds or your appearance, this can be a really easy area of your life to make some positive changes for the sake of your long-term health.

It's usually an eye-opening experience for people to learn that that bar of soap, bottle of shampoo, tube of toothpaste, household cleaner, laundry detergent, air freshener, and on and on is not keeping them healthy, and is actually doing more harm than good.

I know that when you clean all of this up, you and your family will notice a huge difference, even if it's not immediate.

I trust that as a lawyer, you set the bar high for yourself. You work hard to keep up with the ever-changing law, to continue to develop your area of expertise, and to advise your client(s) in the best way you know how. Why not set the bar high when it comes to your own health and that of your family?

As you continue to work through the steps in a BALANCED Way™ and set the bar high in terms of your own health and well-being, I predict you're going to feel increasingly unstoppable and confident in your journey. Keep doing your morning pages, make time to slow down and meditate, notice ways that the universe is reminding you that it's got your back. Only two more steps to learn. Keep going.

dirk's corner

The idea of doing cleanses was pretty foreign to me before we started researching ways to help Cinco. As usual, Bev led the way. I think that must be the norm with husbands and wives. In general, it seems that wives are usually the pioneers and end up having to drag their husbands along. Sometimes that goes well, and sometimes they end up leading entirely different lifestyles. We each feel very fortunate that we both became very passionate about holistic wellness.

When we first suggested to Cinco that he do some coffee enemas to help with his struggle, he was pretty much mortified at the idea. I have to admit, I was as well! I wasn't going to ask my father to do anything that I wouldn't do myself though, so I gave it a try. I was so glad that Bev talked me into it. I really could tell a difference in my energy level. This was a couple of months after I started drinking the ionized water correctly, which is fantastic for cleansing, as well. The CE was just one component of the overall program, so I can't really say how much effect it had on my energy level by itself, but altogether I was really starting to feel younger.

Since then we have learned about many other ways to cleanse that Bev mentioned above. We incorporate all of these into our lives periodically, and wouldn't have it any other way now. Regarding the colon cleanses: Just try it. No, the process isn't pleasant, but you'll probably be glad you did.

A wonderful tool to assist you in seeking out the right personal and skin care products is the Environmental Working Group's cosmetics database at www.ewg.org/skindeep. If a product you are researching is not in that database, you can enter it and its ingredients for a rating.

A similar tool that is available as a phone app that you can use is Think Dirty (www.thinkdirtyapp.com). It works similar to the Fooducate app and allows you to scan the bar code of personal and beauty products to see how "dirty" or safe they are.

chapter nine

Exercise

"Physical fitness is not only one of the most important keys to a healthy body, it is the basis of dynamic and creative intellectual activity."

JOHN F. KENNEDY

my friend Juan Cruz owns a law firm where I serve as outside counsel for certain matters. He has a thriving practice, with several full-time lawyers and dozens of public school district clients, as well as private clients. I don't know how he keeps all the plates spinning, but he makes it look easy.

I suspect part of his secret to making it look easy, including always having a pleasant but focused disposition, is that he is an avid runner. I look forward to his early morning Facebook posts when he shares his Map My Run® stats for the day. As a matter of fact, he recently posted from Las Vegas on Easter weekend. Apparently, it is four miles from Wynn to Mandalay Bay.

Now, I don't know about you, but I can promise you that I've never gotten out of bed early in the morning in Vegas, laced up my tennies, and gone for a run. But Juan loves running, that is his thing, and he is dedicated.

You don't have to be a marathoner to maintain a healthy lifestyle, though. You just have to be consistent with whatever form(s) of exercise you choose.

In case you need a refresher course on why you want to get at least some exercise on a consistent basis, here are my Top 10 reasons:

1. Regular physical activity is what really makes the lymphatic system work at its optimum. The lymphatic system has three main functions. The first is to maintain the balance of fluid in the blood versus the tissues. Second, it forms part of the body's immune system and helps defend against and eliminate foreign bodies such as bacteria. Third, it facilitates absorption of fats and fat-soluble nutrients in the digestive system. It's kind of a big deal.

2. Physical activity also causes sweating, which flushes toxins out of your body. As I mentioned, you don't have to be a marathoner. Walking, bicycling, yoga, and dancing are a few great choices for helping you get your sweat on, and it's good to mix them up.

3. Regular exercise helps to improve sleep. It strengthens circadian rhythms, which helps provide alertness during the day and bring on sleep at night. During exercise, a wide variety of biochemicals are released in the body and the brain. This affects the body's internal clock mechanisms and helps promote regular sleeping patterns. You need your rest, especially during this time of transition in your life.

4. Exercise is also a great way to practice regularly setting and achieving goals. For example, when you set a goal to exercise for a set amount of time and then you achieve that goal, you are training yourself to do the same in other areas of your life. By setting exercise intentions and then following through, you are engaging in an activity that will positively spill over into other areas of your life.

5. Regular exercise makes people happier. Studies have shown that people who exercise regularly experience greater levels of excitement and enthusiasm than those who don't. In one study, reported happiness levels following exercise were second only to reported levels following sex. Which, of course, can also be a fun way to exercise.

6. Exercising can also give you an energy boost and fight fatigue. Although exercising when fatigued seems like it would just tire you more, it has

actually been shown to do the opposite as long as you don't overdo it. Researchers at the University of Georgia discovered that low-intensity exercise resulted in a 20 percent boost in energy and 65 percent lower levels of fatigue. High-intensity exercise resulted in only a 40 percent drop in fatigue. A little exercise is a much better and healthier way to overcome fatigue than reaching for an energy drink or other caffeinated beverage.

7. Although this seems obvious, I also want to remind you of the importance of exercise in increasing strength, endurance, and flexibility. Stretching, strength training, and cardio are all important. Stretching increases your flexibility and helps prevent muscle injuries. Strength training not only increases your muscle size and strength, it helps keep your bones stronger as well. Cardio has a host of benefits including better endurance, improved detoxification, and better cardiovascular health.

8. Regular exercise has been shown to increase the size of the hippocampus, which is the area of the brain that controls memory and learning. You know how important that is in this profession.

9. Want to improve your self-confidence? Being in good physical shape is one of the biggest factors in having a positive self-image, which contributes highly towards confidence levels. Merely the act

of exercise itself contributes to better self-image, regardless of fitness level. Simply getting exercise has an effect on how we view ourselves.

10. Even just five minutes of aerobic exercise has been shown to reduce anxiety and stress. People who exercise before work or during their lunch break experience lower levels of stress and increased productivity at their job than those who do not. You want to be at your best in terms of job performance when embarking on a new career journey.

Don't Worry; Be Happy

We've already discussed at length the fact that the legal profession isn't the healthiest. And I don't have to tell you that unhealthy levels of stress are a plague in this profession. Let's take a closer look at some reasons why you absolutely, positively have to manage that.

Stress is one of the biggest factors contributing to poor health. It has been shown to help cancer cells survive in animal tests.

A study at Yale University showed that stressful occasions can actually shrink brain size in areas tied to emotion and physiological functions. According to research in the journal *Molecular Psychiatry*, stress can also contribute to the shortening of telomeres and speed up aging.

Sustained stress can also cause depression, and people who are more stressed out about the stresses of everyday life are much more likely to have chronic health issues than those who deal with everyday stresses in a more relaxed manner.

How Much?

The World Health Organization's recommended weekly minimum amount of time for exercise is 30 minutes a day, five days a week. Below that, the rates of disease and morbidity increase significantly. And the amount of exercise that has the greatest benefit in terms of decreased rates of disease and morbidity is an hour a day, seven days a week. Above that, there is no increased benefit.

Researchers don't know the exact process of how exercise boosts immunity, but it clearly has an effect on reduction of disease. If you want to live a longer life with a higher quality of life, sufficient exercise is a critical component.

Interval Training

Interval training can be a great way to burn calories and fat, and will do it in a shorter time period than "regular" exercising. I recommend incorporating a little of it in your exercise routine. In a nutshell, it's a mix of alternating high-intensity bursts of exercise with low-intensity recovery periods in between. For example, instead of jogging at a steady pace for 30 minutes, try sprinting for 20 seconds, and then jogging or walking for 30 seconds. Then repeat for the duration of your workout.

Exercising in this manner means your heart rate will be at its maximum more than if you were exercising steadily at a lower intensity. This, in turn, will cause your body to burn fat and calories at a much faster rate. It also will stimulate your adrenal glands to release adrenaline, resulting in a euphoric feeling known as the "runner's high." The duration of the burst periods and rest periods don't really matter too much. Just structure it so that your rest periods of lower intensity are slightly longer than the high-intensity bursts.

Body Weight Training

Body weight training is simply working out while using your own body weight in the routine. Exercises such as sit-ups, push-ups, pull-ups, leg lifts, squats, etc. fall into this category. It's an excellent way to tone your body that can be done anywhere, and you don't need any special equipment.

Incorporating the interval training principles into a body-weight training routine is also a very effective way to maximize the results of your workout. However, instead of making the rest periods longer as with a high-cardio activity such as sprinting, make them equal. For example, do sit-ups for 30 seconds, then rest for 30 seconds, and so on. If you mix it up with exercises that work out all the parts of your body, you can get a great full-body workout in a relatively short period of time.

Yoga

Yoga is so important for a variety of reasons, including helping increase your body's core strength. It's also helpful for your body to recover from injuries, as well as the prevention of re-injuring old ones. In fact, yoga is beneficial in all areas of fitness including flexibility, cardiorespiratory fitness, muscle strength, and body composition. It feels so good. If you've never been to a yoga class, I encourage you to attend a small, beginner class near you. Remember that you're not in competition with anyone. Breathe. Enjoy. Ahhh....

Get Outside

In Chapter 4, we talked about getting outside in nature. It's worth repeating. Weather permitting, I encourage you to exercise outside during the daylight on a regular basis. Among other reasons we've already talked about, vitamin D is a critical component of maintaining optimum health and warding off illness. You may be concerned about sun exposure, and rightfully so. Remember, though, that the sun is your friend in moderate doses. Wear protective clothing and/or try to use natural sunscreen. You can even make your own, non-toxic sunscreen. That's what I do.

Exercising Indoors

When the weather doesn't cooperate or when you have other reasons for indoor exercise, you can find tons of helpful videos online. You can also try a rebounder, which is basically a small trampoline. Rebounders are a fantastic and inexpensive way to get a good low-impact cardio workout. Being relatively small, they are perfect for using in the home, the office, or even when traveling. You can also add a stabilizing bar for more stability during a workout.

Other options for indoor exercise include attending a yoga or other exercise or dance class at a local gym, YMCA, or community college.

Be Consistent

What matters is consistency. For lots of people, hiring a personal trainer or having an exercise partner/accountability buddy is the key to consistency. If you're not a person who already has a regular exercise program, decide on a set period of time for one and stick with it for that amount of time, whether that's a month, six weeks, or longer. Decide in advance, and don't give up.

Have Fun!

Whatever you decide to establish as your routine, whether it's hitting the gym in the morning, starting a walking group with your neighbors, taking dance lessons, riding a bicycle, or all of the above, make sure it is fun. If you don't enjoy it, you are not going to stick with the program. The good news is, even if you think you don't really like exercise or think you don't have time for it, there are so many ways to make it fun and find time for it.

So, get moving, have fun, and don't forget to jot down how you're feeling in your BALANCED Way™ journal.

dirk's corner

Getting enough exercise has usually not been a problem for me. I was an athlete in school, and have always loved hiking, kayaking, and cycling. My Adventure Club business gave Bev and me more than enough opportunities to get exercise.

Life happens, though, and at this point in mine, I do have periods of time when I don't exercise enough. And I can feel it. It's funny, because Bev and I both seem to notice being sluggish at the same time, after so many days of being attached to our computers and not getting enough exercise. Sometimes we just have to set things aside and get out for a walk or a bike ride. I am glad to have someone who likes it as much as I do.

As Bev has said, we ended our RTW about two-thirds of the way into it because I injured my knee. We wrote this book during my healing and recovery time. Because of the nature of the injury, I was not able to get nearly as much exercise as I had in the past. And I felt the difference. So, I had to adapt and find ways to exercise that helped strengthen my knee while not putting demands on it. It's amazing how big of a difference it made in my recovery.

I recommend slipping in exercise, like taking the stairs when possible and parking in the space farthest away from the building. Walk or bike short distances that you would normally drive.

If you decide to join an exercise program or hiking club, Meetup.com is great for this. You can also make a game out of exercise, to make sure you stick with it. Try using a phone app or other way of tracking physical activity.

A good way to start your day off is to set a goal of completing a short exercise routine when you first get out of bed in the morning, before you will "reward" yourself with that first cup of coffee, tea, or whatever else is part of your morning ritual.

chapter ten
Decide Your Path Forward

"It doesn't matter which side of the fence you get off on sometimes. What matters most is getting off. You cannot make progress without making decisions."

JIM ROHN

We've covered a lot of ground in these pages, and there's one last step for you to master. It is actually the most important step in the whole BALANCED Way™ program, and that is to Decide Your Path Forward.

Let that sink in. This is what everything else has prepared you for. You can decide what's best for you.

If you just got a big lump in your throat, don't fret. Just take it one day at a time and work your way up to making your big decision when you're ready.

Start by Doing More Things that Scare You

If you've been playing it safe your whole life, like the old me, work on getting used to stepping out of your comfort zone. That advice you've heard countless times to do what scares you – actually works.

You can do this by:

- Enlisting support, especially from those who have already done the things that scare you.

- Adopting the outlook of Tim Ferriss, self-help entrepreneur and best-selling author of *The Four-Hour Workweek*. Ferriss says that fear is your friend; "that sometimes fear lets you know what you shouldn't do, but more often than not, it tells you exactly what you should do. Making the decision that you're going to do something in spite of your fear can be empowering and can take you exactly where you need to be."

- Asking yourself, what's the worst thing that could happen? We have learned to fear for good reason. Throughout our evolution, fear has kept us from doing things that are harmful or unsafe. In our modern times, though, fear can keep us from doing the very things that our soul feels compelled to do. That creates inner conflict, which causes us to feel frustrated, angry, and paralyzed.

- Considering who you know who has done that thing that scares you and has survived. This will help you distinguish between rational and irrational fears.

- Starting small. Flying on an airplane is super scary for some people, while others make a hobby out of jumping out of them. Start by doing things that are just outside of your comfort zone if that's what's needed to get you to do something. Make a habit of doing increasingly scary stuff on a regular basis.

When you regularly do what scares you, you become empowered to do so many things you might have thought were impossible before. That's one of the things that gets you the life you've always wanted.

Get Risky

So let's look at some options that are available to you when it comes to taking a risk with your career. I'm sure you can think of others, but here are some ideas to get your wheels turning.

1. If you know you need to make a change but don't want to leave the legal profession altogether, you can decide to make a move to another law firm or other entity. This option might be right for you if you:

- Enjoy practicing law, but you're not enjoying the firm where you're currently working or are concerned about its sustainability.

- Find the work you do interesting but don't want to work such long hours.

- Feel you're underpaid in your current job and can earn more doing the same or similar work somewhere else.

- Are satisfied with your level of pay but are bored with your area of practice.

- Feel micromanaged.

- Are tired of working after hours and/or on weekends.

- Feel like your work has no meaning, and you want to do something that makes a difference in people's lives.

- Are tired of working with incompetent people.

- Want to spend more time with your family, and your current position doesn't allow for that.

- Just want a fresh start somewhere else.

2. You can leave the practice of law altogether. This might be the right decision for you if you:

- Find that practicing law isn't as interesting as you had hoped.

- Hate going to work every day.

- Have a hard time getting out of bed to go to work but have plenty of energy for other things in your life.

- Have insomnia, especially on Sunday nights.

- Start feeling down on Saturday afternoon, already dreading Monday morning.

- Feel physically sick when you think of work.

- Have no interest in law and never really think about it or read about it outside of work.

- Spend much of your workday avoiding work, choosing instead to surf the net, read the news, or make personal phone calls.

- Fantasize about doing something else, especially if you fantasize about doing *anything* else.

- Change the subject when someone asks you what you do.

- Feel like your legal career is not at all reflective of who you really are.

- Stay in the profession only because you need the income.

- See no connection between the work that you do and actually helping people as you want to.

3. If you want to keep practicing law and you enjoy your area of practice but aren't satisfied with your current situation, you can start your own firm, whether solo or with other lawyers. This might be the right decision for you if you:

- Have always wanted to start your own business.

- Don't like having a supervisor.

- Want flexibility so you can spend more time with your family, for travel, or for other pursuits.

- Want to have more control over the clients you accept and your caseload.

- Have trusted colleagues with whom you'd like to practice.

- Want a non-traditional practice, like one that allows you to work from home or other location-independent situation.

4. You can go back to school, either to earn your LLM or to study something other than law. It doesn't even have to be university-level coursework. What certifications or other trainings could you acquire to work, even if just temporarily or part-time, in an industry that you're really passionate about?

Sit with these ideas for a while, and think of your own. Get a drink of water, ask your inner voice, listen for the answers, and keep journaling about thoughts, ideas, and fears that come to mind. This part of the process, just like the other steps, isn't meant to happen in one day. You've invested this much time not knowing what to do. Give yourself time to feel confident that you know what to do. Trust that the universe is conspiring in your favor to provide answers, opportunities, and people who can help you.

It's important to remember that, even if you're that person who is almost in tears on the way to work and maybe falling asleep on the way home, you are on the right track. Please honor and reward yourself for the progress you're already making by even considering making some of these radical changes in your life.

A Graceful Departure

If you ultimately decide that the best decision for you is to leave your current job, I know you'll want to make sure you do that the right way: gracefully, ethically, and on your terms.

It can be harder than you thought to leave your job, even if you have grown to despise it. You're potentially leaving behind co-workers and clients you've enjoyed working with and have spent years of your life with. You're potentially leaving behind a steady paycheck and other benefits that you and your family have relied upon. And fear of the unknown in and of itself can keep you up at night wondering if you're making a mistake.

If you are walking away from a position with a company or entity that meets your high level of integrity, that makes it even harder than leaving behind a position where part of you wants to yell, "Take this job and shove it!" or act out that scene from the movie *Office Space*.

Here are some strategies:

- Make a plan that takes into account responsibilities that you have – towards your family, your employer, yourself, and your creditors.

- Set priorities to help you stay focused and on track, as you wind things down and prepare for your new adventure.

- Expect the unexpected, especially if you're transitioning into self-employment. It never goes as smoothly or as quickly as you think it will.

- For more help transitioning your work, I highly recommend you pick up Jeanne Boschert's *The Ethical Exit*. It is a quick read that is full of practical tools.

Whatever you decide your path forward is, I want you to know that there are others who've walked into the unknown, and who are thriving today.

I'd like to introduce you to some of them.

Alexis

I told you about Alexis in Chapter 5. She is the author of the best-selling book, *Wear Clean Underwear!: A Fast, Fun, Friendly – and Essential – Guide to Legal Planning for Busy Parents* and owner of the New Law Business Model™. Her business offers a unique, systemized, and client-centered approach that helps lawyers fall in love with their careers again. She also focuses on the business side of lawyering, which I certainly didn't learn in law school. I'll bet you didn't either.

Alexis will tell you she didn't grow up in a wealthy family, and she definitely has had some challenges during her lifetime that easily could have taken her down an entirely different path. Thank goodness she didn't let any of those challenges stop her from becoming the lawyer and businessperson that she is today.

She graduated first in her class from Georgetown Law School, clerked for a federal judge in Miami, and then landed a job at one of the top law firms in the country in Los Angeles. Pretty much as soon as she started that job, she was unhappy because she felt there was a huge disconnect between what she had dreamed about when she went to law school and the reality of being a lawyer.

Alexis had dreamed about going to law school and coming out and making a difference in people's lives; but in reality, she felt that practice in that law firm was totally transactional and not relational at all. Sure, she was earning a six-figure income, and most people would agree that she had a very successful legal career from the start. They'd be right. But she knew something was missing very early on.

Among other things, she was missing out on some of the joys of being a mom of young kids. She identified that there was little opportunity for advancement in the big firm where she worked, assuming she wanted to keep doing the type of law she really wanted to practice, which is estate planning. Alexis left the big firm world and thought about leaving the practice of law altogether. Instead, she decided to bring back the Personal Family Lawyer® relationship. She started her own practice with that concept in mind.

Taking only a few clients with her, Alexis grew her own practice to the point of bringing in $1 million a year in revenue and certainly appeared to be the epitome of success once again. Unfortunately, she learned the hard way that the way she built her practice was not sustainable because – like most lawyers

– she needed to learn how to run it like a business. It took a near-death experience on a Los Angeles freeway to get her to make some changes in her life and career. Along the way, she also ended up taking another hard look at her practice and making more much-needed changes.

Today Alexis owns a thriving business, sees a handful of clients when she wants to, and mostly works from home. She oversees a team of 22 and also teaches other lawyers how to practice law in a way that is truly rewarding for the lawyers she works with and their clients. What a concept.

Alexis is also the creator of a program called the Money Map to Freedom™, which helps people identify and get what they "really, really, really, REALLY" want out of life. It's a fascinating and eye-opening program that, by the time you've worked through the BALANCED Way™ process, will help you take your life to places you may never have thought were possible. For more information about the Money Map to Freedom™ program, email us at info@balanced-way.com.

Alexis has started a movement. I'm thrilled to be a part of that same movement, serving small businesses by working alongside them as their trusted advisor, as well as working with families in legal life planning. You might refer to this as estate planning, but it's so much more than that, the way we do it.

Before deciding to start the New Law Business Model™, Alexis might have been scared to death, but she took action. And that is what makes all the difference.

Juan

In Chapter 9, I told you about my friend Juan. He and I met almost 20 years ago, when we were both associates at the same firm. Like Alexis, Juan is an incredible businessperson, in addition to being an outstanding lawyer. I'm honored to be affiliated with his firm, J. Cruz & Associates; and I'm thankful to have called him my friend for all these years.

As I told you before, Juan works hard. Representing public school districts, as well as other governmental entities, means he is often working late at night, attending board meetings and/or traveling to the next one. Everyone in his firm works hard, shares a lot of the same attributes, and they are all incredibly supportive of one another. Being affiliated with Juan's firm is like being part of a family, and Juan fosters that.

Like many of us imagined in law school, Juan thought his daily life as a lawyer would entail a lot of time in the courtroom involved in litigation. However, it didn't turn out that way for him. He began his career in an insurance defense firm, spending most of his time writing legal memos. He jumped ship pretty early to government entity defense because it got him into the courtroom, which is what he thought he was looking for at the time. But he soon became bored of the routine accident cases. When the opportunity presented itself to move into school law, he jumped on it and found his calling.

Juan's a health nut like me, and – despite his tireless work ethic – he still makes sure he sets aside time in his life for himself, for his family, for travel, and for his personal relationships. He is an avid runner, as I mentioned in Chapter 9, rising early most mornings to run at least a few miles before work. He also practices yoga several times weekly, and it is his go-to activity for calming himself down after a long day's work. He closes Friday afternoons with a hot yoga class to end the week with some peacefulness.

I'm sure it was scary or at least very uncomfortable for him to walk away from the firm where he and I met so many years ago. There were, undoubtedly, lots of reasons not to do it. He did it anyway. He worked for the law firm where we met for a long time, but knew deep down that he wanted to have his own firm. Once he had developed a large enough client base, he decided to branch out on his own. He knew it was risky, but was confident he could make it work.

Since finding the area of practice that he really resonates with, he has continued to achieve success after success. It's now been four years since Juan started his own firm, which has become one of the top school law firms in the state of Texas. The highlight for him so far was arguing a case before the Texas Supreme Court in 2015. He spent months in preparation, memorizing 50 cases that were pertinent to the issues he would be arguing before the Court, plus a whole set of statutory and constitutional laws. His diligence paid off, and the Court rendered a unanimous favorable decision for his client. Way to go, Juan!

Along the way, Juan has learned how important it is to maintain balance in his life as a lawyer. Placing boundaries in regards to time and clients has helped him have a personal and professional life. He has also hired more associates to be able to have some more time off to spend with family and friends. Although he loves practicing law, it is very clear to him that his work will not define him at the end of his life. He wants to be remembered by how he treated others and the personal relationships he had, rather than his professional accomplishments.

To Juan, the practice of law is about finding solutions to people's problems and somehow making their worries go away. He gets great satisfaction in closing out a case or project with good results, because he knows that on the other end there must be someone who does not have to stay up late at night thinking about their problem.

Juan has clearly got that happy/healthy lawyer thing down.

Danielle

My friend Danielle is not a lawyer, but I'd be remiss if I didn't tell you about her. She's an excellent example of someone who left behind a lucrative, comfortable job with benefits and started anew, on her own terms. Danielle is from Chicago, but I met her on the Wild Coast of South Africa in 2016. She was the yoga instructor at a hostel where Dirk and I stayed along with our friend Scott.

Talk about doing what scares you. Danielle encouraged me to do a cliff jump in South Africa. What an adrenaline rush that was! I have to admit, though, the scariest thing Danielle has encouraged me to do, and she doesn't even know it, is expanding my legal practice at a time when it was not the easiest or most comfortable decision to make.

She knows what it feels like to do what scares her.

Three years ago, Danielle quit her full-time job with a good salary. She was drained, stressed, unfulfilled, and unsatisfied. She felt like she'd done all of the things she was supposed to do to be successful according to society's standards. She had two degrees, a "great job with benefits" and a nice apartment in the city, but she still craved something more. She had completed a yoga teacher certification and a Reiki healing certification, and was still unsure about what she was meant to do with her life.

Before she left her "great job," Danielle would sit at her desk and daydream about living a life of travel, freedom, and fulfillment. She lived vicariously through her favorite Facebook profiles and Instagram accounts while feeling stuck in her own life.

The beginning of her short-lived career working for an Urban and Public Affairs Program seemed good enough. As you might be able to relate to, she was grateful to have a job with steady income and vacation days. But the newness wore off fairly quickly, and she began to feel like she was just going through the motions. She realized that she needed more creative freedom and opportunity for growth in her work. Over time she started to grow increasingly bored and tired of the administrative nature of her work, and she lost her enthusiasm.

The biggest aha moment for Danielle came when she asked for a raise. She thought more money would make her happier, but all of the hoops that she had to jump through made it impossible for her to get the raise. This was after she had taken a trip to Costa Rica and gotten a taste of what life could be like in nature in the Caribbean.

As it turned out, Danielle is grateful that she didn't get the raise, because not getting it made her decide to quit and move to Costa Rica. In hindsight, she realizes no amount of money could have made her happier working the job that she was working. It just wasn't a good fit for her. Danielle says that she can now clearly see how quitting her job and moving to another country expanded her sense of creativity and allowed her to use her passions, unique gifts, and natural talents.

Within three years of quitting her job, Danielle has traveled to 15 countries and four continents, teaching yoga and leading and participating in retreats. She hasn't looked back.

Danielle also values her health as one of her greatest assets. She feels fortunate to live in a place where exercise and eating clean are naturally a part of her healthy lifestyle. She bikes or walks everywhere, and she swims in the ocean daily. She also eats the freshest healthy local fruits and vegetables, many of which are superfoods that grow wild in Costa Rica. She practices and teaches yoga regularly, which also keeps her fit.

Danielle has parlayed her passions and talents into becoming a Freedom Lifestyle Strategist©, "helping freedom-seeking souls to live their life purpose and become the best version of themselves." She teaches workshops and leads yoga retreats in beautiful places like Costa Rica, Bali, and back in South Africa.

Like the lawyers mentioned above, she is such an inspiration and a wonderful reminder of how magical life can be when you face your fears and decide to live your life on your own terms. We hope to see you right alongside us at one of her retreats. Pura vida!

You've Got the Tools!

And, there you have it: all 8 Steps of the BALANCED Way™ to having the career – and life – of your dreams, topped off with a lot of inspiration.

Now that you have all the tools to get clear on what you really want – to have the stamina, and physical and mental well-being to go after it, and to approach your new adventure with confidence, grace, and dignity – I want you to imagine what your life will look like six months to a year from now.

Again, sit with that for a while, take a walk outside, ask you inner voice, dare to dream, and know that you can be that happy lawyer that you were born to be.

You've earned it. Well done!

~~~

dirk's corner

Ultimately, no matter what you do to prepare yourself for a big life or career change, you will need to make some decisions and act on them. That is often the hardest part of the process for many people. When Bev decided to depart the world of corporate law in pursuit of a different career path, it was not an easy decision for her to make. It meant leaving a secure position and stepping away from a profession that she had lived and breathed for over 15 years to take a big risk. Her sons were at the forefront of her thoughts, and she did not take any of it lightly.

But that decision of Bev's led us both down a trail of discovery that we are still on today. The retail brick-and-mortar part of our health and wellness business lasted for two years, but we have continued down that path and will apply what we've learned for life. When asked, we love helping others reach their goals and change their lives for the better, too.

Bev has also returned to the practice of law in a way that suits her much better. The corporate lawyer that was in my life for a couple of years wasn't nearly as much fun as the happy lawyer who has now taken her place. And that makes me very happy, as well!

If you want even more inspiration, I recommend you watch the Art Williams *Just Do It 1987* clip on YouTube that's just under three minutes. Art Williams was inspiring people to "just do it" before it was a thing. As of this writing, the video is at this link: https://youtu.be/ARk8QLdnZ6w. If that link doesn't work, just search for it. If you've seen it before, watch it again!

As Bev mentioned, reach out to us at info@balanced-way.com to learn how you can create your own Money Map to Freedom™ and get what you "really, really, really, REALLY want."

And, here's a little trick that may help when facing decisions. Flip a coin. However, instead of letting the coin toss determine your decision, just take note of how you *hope* the coin lands.

Finally, I encourage you to incorporate one of Steve Jobs' most well-known quotes into your life: *"I have looked in the mirror every morning and asked myself: 'If today were the last day of my life, would I want to do what I am about to do today?' And whenever the answer has been 'No' for too many days in a row, I know I need to change something."*

chapter eleven
Embrace the Journey!

"We are at our very best, and we are happiest, when we are fully engaged in work we enjoy on the journey toward the goal we've established for ourselves. It gives meaning to our time off and comfort to our sleep. It makes everything else in life so wonderful, so worthwhile."

EARL NIGHTINGALE

I hope you're feeling as excited for yourself as I am feeling for you right now. I remember being that lawyer who saw a glimmer of hope when my inner voice gave me permission to leave my corporate counsel job. I gave way more notice than anyone would've expected of me, which gave me lots of time to wrap things up and know I was leaving on good terms. Every day from the day I gave my notice until my last day there, I walked with a little more spring in my step. On my last day, I wore a floral silk skirt, a casual top, sandals, and my toe ring. I felt like such a rebel!

But you should've seen me during the time that I was working up the courage to walk away.

"I'm not a quitter," I would tell Dirk.

"I know I can stick this out." I'd say that, too, as I vacillated about my big decision.

I mean, there were so many reasons not to leave that job.

Like….

What will my family think?

My sons mean everything to me, and I'd always wanted to be a mom they could be proud of. I was so worried about failing them, and it broke my heart knowing this wouldn't be the first time.

And what about my own mom? Ever since my dad passed away, I'd wanted my mom not to have to worry about money. Yet here I was, contemplating walking away from a well-paying job, having fallen far short of that goal. I didn't make it to the point of paying off all of my debt so that I could then ease her burdens financially. That bothered me a lot.

I had really wanted to be the lawyer success story of my own family, and I was sure I was letting them all down by not being the person who could hack it.

And then….

What would my lawyer friends think if I changed professions?

I was walking away from a very good law job, to do what? To open a woo-woo, holistic wellness center? Would they think I'd joined a cult? Would they ever take me seriously again? I'd worked hard to develop a solid reputation in the legal profession. I had been at it a long time and was not getting any younger. I was deeply invested, and now I was just … walking away?

And then.…

What if I failed again?

And then.…

What if I succeeded? Who would this new wellness guru be? What new friends would I have to make? How many more new things would I have to learn? Would I be shamed if I was caught not following my own advice? What if I learned the hard way that it doesn't really work anyway? (It does work if you want it to, BTW.)

And then back to my family and my lawyer friends.…

How could I ever tell anyone that I was inspired by, hmmm, dead/not-really-dead people who in a way feel like my own trusted advisors? That my dad had never failed me, and I had to trust that he wasn't failing me now? My family wouldn't believe me, and I could never tell them. It would only embarrass them anyway.

I also just knew that if word got out that I was that *out there*, I could never go back to practicing law. I'd be ridiculed, shamed, ostracized. Especially if I failed yet again.

And then.…

What about coming up with financing for our new business? Had we really tapped into enough capital? That could be a whole other book, and that worried me to no end.

It felt horrible to feel like that, to say the least.

But then....

All those thoughts were not as horrible as the thought of staying stuck in a job that I knew was not for me. And, although it was paying the bills, although my family and I were blessed by that opportunity, that job was not for my family, either, because I was not able to give them all of me. That never sits well.

And then....

I remember going to dinner with a group of ladies, and we all took turns complaining and talking about everything that was wrong in our lives. When I chimed in, I talked about how horrible I felt, how I was taking things out on Dirk, how I was so edgy with my kids, how I fantasized about slashing a particular person's tires in the parking lot at work, and on and on. Maybe I needed a hysterectomy, I reasoned aloud, because I felt so sick even though I was supposedly well, and this was clearly not me.

One of the women replied, "What if it *is* you?"

"Excuse me?"

"What if it turns out, you're actually a bitch?" She took a sip of her martini, and we all got quiet for a minute.

"Wow," I thought. "Did she really just say that?"

Then I had an epiphany: I didn't have to choose the way that question made me feel. I didn't have to wonder if she was right or wrong, worrying another day about whether I'd become *that* person. Or worrying for the sake of worrying, about … everything. I could, instead, in my own quiet and confident way, simply choose to be happy.

And that's how I pushed through my fears and started my new life. No matter how many reasons I listed for why I should stay at that job and keep managing my life the same way I'd done for years, none of them outweighed the thought that, at the end of the day, I had a choice about how I show up in this world. And the choices I'd been making all those years were making me, and all too often those around me, miserable.

I started really listening to my inner voice, knowing it had always served me well when I did. I stopped resisting and searching for answers outside of myself, and I *allowed*. I chose to keep the best parts of my life and gracefully bid adieu to the parts that no longer served me or my loved ones.

Once I remembered I could do it, I was all in; and I never wavered again. I have never regretted taking my life in a whole new direction on many levels. I will tell you, things got a little rough financially for a while. But I remained committed to a new way of living.

I am still committed … to being happy and making decisions daily that support a healthy, relaxed lifestyle. To valuing my health and my happiness as two of my greatest assets (which are really one), no matter which hat I'm wearing.

It's not all beach bliss, although I'd be lying if I didn't say a lot of it actually is. Don't hate me for that. If it sounds like your dream come true, go after it.

Since I made what I call my big decision, Dirk and I have started a few successful businesses, traveled the world, and I have returned – happily at last – to the law business. I am so fortunate that I get to coach people to reach their health and life goals (that's the teacher in me), while still practicing law in a way that my legal clients and I love.

As my cup runneth over, I am blessed more than I deserve with a loving husband and three amazing, really cool grown sons. It gives me tremendous joy to spend time with them almost whenever we want, especially when we get to travel together around the world.

Life is no longer a struggle, but it took a huge leap of faith to get out of that mindset. There were times when our family did not have this love fest going on.

Your Big Decision

When you decide your path forward, you'll undoubtedly face many of these same obstacles and fears I did. I'm not going to lie to you. It's going to suck some days. Some of the BALANCED Way™ steps are going to feel like they are kicking your butt at times, like you are not BALANCED at all in that moment, and you will wonder why you signed on for this. You will wonder what this has to do with lawyering at all.

That final step, though, that part about actually believing in yourself and deciding to take that leap of faith and choosing what serves you, that's the best-feeling step. All the others will lead you to it and get you through it.

I believe you know deep down, just as I did, that staying stuck is not an option. Turning your back on the person and the lawyer you were born to be is not an option.

You deserve to become that happy lawyer you were born to be. Your family deserves for you to become that person, too.

I hope you choose happiness.

Stay on this path, and give it a try.

What's the alternative?

conclusion

Welcome to your new life!

You now have effective tools to help you land your dream job right away, or to develop a game plan to go after it within a period of time that you decide upon. You also now have effective tools to start a new life and not just a new job – if you want it – with greater confidence, purpose, vitality, and HAPPINESS than you may ever have imagined.

As you continue your journey, I hope you'll remember that you're an original, and that you'll continue to feel empowered to claim your space in the world and push on. The world needs you.

As I've told you, I'm on a mission to change the way lawyers serve their communities, their families, and themselves. I want healthy, happy lawyers – and the clients we serve – to be the norm and not the exception. I hope you'll join the movement.

It's always a joy to watch lawyers in transition get clear on their highest purpose, get healthy, and start showing up in the world in the way they were meant to. Dirk and I look forward to reading your stories. Please share them with us at info@balanced-way.com.

Everyone's journey is unique and beautiful, and we both thank you for allowing us to be a part of yours.

Namaste.

acknowledgements

there must be a thousand reasons why this book might never have been written, including not having enough time, not knowing where to begin, and … inertia.

Thankfully, the universe and a whole lot of people conspired to make it happen, for which we are eternally grateful.

Mallie, Cinco, and Dad, you left us sooner than we wanted you to, but without your inspiration and guidance, our lives would not have gone down a path that eventually led to this book. Thank you.

Johnnie Mae, thanks for all your support in so many ways. We never could have done this without you.

DeLynn, Rochelle, Courtney, Nicole, and Jordan, thanks for sparking this endeavor. Your requests for advice are what inspired us to write this book now, instead of waiting for the "right time." We hope it provides answers to at least some of your questions.

To the Morgan James Publishing team: Special thanks to David Hancock, CEO & Founder for believing in us and our message. To my Author Relations Manager, Gayle West, thanks for making the process seamless and easy. Many more thanks to everyone else, but especially Jim Howard, Bethany Marshall, and Nickcole Watkins.

Angela Lauria, you had us at "Write a book that makes a difference." Your "Keep Writing Forward" mantra and unwavering certainty that we would get this book finished kept us … well … writing forward, no matter what. Thank you.

Maggie McReynolds, thank you for your patience and superb editing expertise. You held our hands just the right amount, and kept encouraging and helping us say what we wanted to say.

Danielle Miller, branding expert extraordinaire, thank you for helping us nail the title and subtitle. The title alone gives lawyers reason to smile, and that's a great place to start a movement.

Alexis Neely, we were destined to meet on this journey. Thank you for your determination to return lawyering to its rightful place as a helping profession, and for sharing your vision to help lawyers serve families and businesses as the trusted advisors we are meant to be.

Juan Cruz, working with you all these years has always felt like working with family. Thank you for your commitment to excellence and, most importantly, for your friendship.

Danielle Ashe, thank you for your steadfastness to staying true to your innermost being and inspiring others to do the same. We'll see you again, doing something adventurous and awesome, in the not-too-distant future.

Thanks to Mom, Gerard, Steven, Nick, Melissa, Travis, and the rest of our family for being patient with us when we came home early from our world travels; and, instead of spending as much time as we would've liked catching up and creating new memories, we went to work on this book and on our businesses. Thank you for holding space for us to continue to evolve into the people we are meant to be in this life. We love you.

about the authors

beverly and Dirk Davidek are the creators of the BALANCED Way™ program (www.Balanced-Way.com). Beverly has been learning how to strike the balance as an attorney since 1994, and Dirk has been an entrepreneur focused on helping busy professionals carve out time for themselves since 2002. In addition, together, they have a combined 18 years in the health and wellness industry. Their mission is to teach lawyers and other busy professionals learn how to meet the mental and physical demands of their careers in a purposeful, fulfilling way. Their home base is New Braunfels, Texas, but they are world travelers, frequently on the move. When home in Texas, they enjoy spending time with their moms and three grown sons.

Throughout her legal career, Beverly's practice areas have included family law, criminal law, insurance defense, school law, employment law, estate planning, business law, and corporate law. She also served as an Assistant District Attorney prosecuting child abuse and neglect cases. Her varied background gives her a unique perspective on the challenges many lawyers face when searching for the right job. Years of practice have also taught her to approach law in a relational way, rather than a strictly transactional way, and she coaches other lawyers to do the same. As owner of Davidek Law Firm, PLLC (www.DavidekLaw.com), her current practice areas include special education, legal life planning for families, and outsourced general counsel for life coaches and other small businesses.

Beverly is also an entrepreneur in the health and wellness industry, having co-owned and -operated a holistic wellness center based in San Antonio, Texas, with her husband Dirk. She holds certifications as a personal development coach, nutrition coach, blood microscopist, raw food chef, and ThetaHealing® practitioner. An admitted essential oils junkie, Beverly has a thriving essential oils business, which she balances with her busy coaching and law businesses.

Beverly's greatest accomplishment has been raising three phenomenal gentlemen who remind her every day, without saying a word, why she does what she does.

A certified fun junkie, Dirk has been a successful restaurateur, entrepreneur in the event planning and adventure travel industries, creator of KokoMotion.com, as well as co-owner and -operator of the holistic wellness center that he and Beverly ran with their sons in San Antonio, Texas. Dirk has a BBA from the University of Texas at Austin and holds certifications as a personal development coach, nutrition coach, blood microscopist, blackjack dealer, and downriver kayak instructor.

Dirk's greatest accomplishment has been helping people pursue their passions through Adventure Club San Antonio, which he started in 2002 and sold in 2015. In addition to Beverly and him meeting in the club and getting married, 40-50 other couples met through the club and got married as well during that time. And that has continued under its new owners, who were also one of those couples. Out of those couples, the overwhelming majority are still together. Dirk has a particular knack for helping people connect with each other and live the lives they've always dreamed of.

thank you

hank you so much for reading! The fact that you've made it to this point in the book tells us that you must be ready.

We believe in you. We believe you're ready to have the career and life that you've dreamed of, ready to value your health as your greatest asset as a lawyer, ready to reach your highest potential, and ready to learn how you can have it all without losing your mind.

We're so excited for you!

To support you in your journey and help you get clear on whether your time is now, we've created a "Dream Job Readiness Assessment" for you. It's a simple diagnostic tool to help you identify where your red flags are and what's stopping you from making your dreams come true.

You can get your FREE assessment and our A-Z Wellness Guide at www.happylawyerbook.com.

And there's a Bonus Chapter that you won't want to miss. Written by Dirk, it tells the rest of the story of our health and wellness journey and how we were inspired to make radical, positive changes in our own lives. We hope this will also keep you inspired and moving towards your dreams. You can get it at www.happylawyerbonuschapter.com.

Happy Lawyering!

Morgan James
Speakers Group

www.TheMorganJamesSpeakersGroup.com

We connect Morgan James published
authors with live and online events
and audiences who will benefit
from their expertise.